MW00442371

The Essential Guide To Writing And Selling Production Music

Dr Michael Hewitt

Edited by Juliet Dover

Additional contributions by Ashley Hewitt

Published by Stereo Output Limited, company number 11174059
Please go to www.stereooutput.com to contact us or follow us on
various social media channels.

ISBN-13: 978-1-9996003-1-0

First printing: 2018

**Stereo
Output**

Table of Contents

Introduction

If you are reading this book, it may be because you have an initial interest in production music, but you aren't sure how to take it further. You may be a musician looking for an additional revenue stream. You may have excellent music lying dormant that you don't know what to do with. Alternatively, you may have watched television, heard the music they used, and thought "I could do better!".

Regardless of your reasons for reading, this book will help you.

In comparison with the popular music industry, production music is an industry that remains hidden in the shadows. However, the sums of money flowing through it are extraordinary. As authors, we will uncover its secrets. Within these chapters, we will explore:-

- What production music is
- How it is made
- How it is sold
- How it is used
- How to sell your own production music
- The laws that govern production music

Without further ado, let's discover how the contemporary music industry works, and where production music sits within it.

1: The Music Marketplace

The number of people now writing and producing their own music seems to have significantly increased in comparison with twenty or thirty years ago. One of the main reasons for this is that the development of new technologies has brought the delights of music-making into virtually every home, opening up incredible new opportunities for resourceful composers and music producers to create completely new types, styles and genres of music.

The development of this technology has also meant that we no longer have to be trained at the academy, rely upon professional performers to play our music or depend upon publishing and record companies to get our music out there. If we have the will, the urge and the wherewithal we can now do it all ourselves. Using no more than a computer, a MIDI keyboard and access to suitable music production software, we can compose, record and produce music all from the comfort of our own home.

Having done so, we can then convert that music into an audio file, design suitable artwork for cover art, and then upload it to a marketing platform such as Amazon, where our music can then be put on sale to a potential audience of millions - all in a matter of hours.

OVERSATURATION

For independent composers and music producers this is a dream come true. However, the ease of accessibility to the music production process, coupled with the greater numbers of people wishing to take advantage of it means that there is now a huge amount of new music being produced, much of which still awaits appreciation by an interested listener.

This becomes apparent if we look at some of the statistics. At a 2011 Digital Music Forum West presentation, Kevin King, CEO of social music and media platform MusicHype, announced that there were now over 97 million tracks registered to the Gracenote song database.[1] Suffice to say, at these levels the precise number of tracks available ceases to be important anymore. It is like talking about how many stars there are in the galaxy or hairs on a dog's back. The answer is an awful lot!

Inevitably, this explosion of musical creativity does not come about without certain problems. One such is that increasing numbers of people are hoping to sell their music.

This can be problematic because there are now so

---

[1] 97 Million and Counting, MarsBands, http://www.marsbands.com/2011/10/97-million-and-counting/

many people creating and uploading new music that the marketplace has become completely oversaturated, meaning the consumer is not only spoilt for choice, but the likelihood of their discovering and buying your music is considerably reduced.

NEGLIGIBLE FINANCIAL RETURNS

Another problem is that in the exuberance of our new-found musical freedom we often just put our music out there without a full awareness of the implications of what that actually means. Consequently, the likelihood of receiving a fair financial return for our efforts is seriously marred.

Our eagerness to do this is thoroughly encouraged by those shrewd business people who know how to turn a profit from this explosion of musical creativity. These are the owners of the various streaming services - now worth billions of dollars - who have largely built their businesses upon the willingness of composers and music producers to provide them with an abundance of fresh musical content at little or no cost.

It is a sobering fact to learn that the financial returns that even professional artists can expect from this are often minimal. Songwriter David Crosby recently rallied against payouts from streaming services on Twitter having garnered one million plays, alleging his highest earnings ranged from a paltry $0.019 per song stream from Napster to a pathetic $0.00069 per stream from YouTube.

If you are new to the scene the situation is even worse. First, there is not much likelihood that your tracks will receive one million plays. Secondly, because of your eagerness to be heard, you might not be taking into account the fundamental terms of the business into which you are entering, how that business operates and the true value of the product that you are creating. This means that you then become vulnerable to exploitation.

CONTENT AND VALUE

If you are ever to receive a fair financial reward for the music that you produce, it is vital first of all to understand the essential relationship between content and value. This relationship all hinges upon the fact that when you write a piece of music, you then count as a creator of that particular type of content.

In an age that increasingly relies upon the flow of information, content - of whatever kind - is absolutely crucial to the entire process. It is so crucial in fact, that every type of content that it is possible to imagine now has financial value. And those who know how to exploit and monetize this content do very well from this exploitation.

As creators of musical content, it helps us to know that the product we are creating has its own inherent value within this marketplace. Once we appreciate this, we will then be in a far better position to realize the financial worth of that content. Our ability to do so however will hinge upon our understanding of the fact that it works as a three-stage process. See Fig. 1:

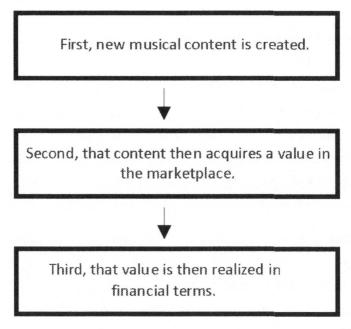

First, new musical content is created.

Second, that content then acquires a value in the marketplace.

Third, that value is then realized in financial terms.

Fig. 1: *Three stages of the realization of the value of musical content*

Central to this is the fact that when you write a piece of music, the law recognizes that piece of music to be a form of property. The law also recognizes that as the music creator, you are the rightful owner of that property. This legally recognized right of ownership confers a tremendous amount of power upon you. This is because you now hold the rights to a product that has value in the marketplace. At this level, music then becomes like any other type of product that can be bought and sold - just like potatoes, bread, diamonds or oil.

As the creator of that content, if you then give it away for free in the hope that somebody will enjoy listening to it, you are in effect transferring the inherent value of that content to the platform that hosts it. The value of that platform then increases in direct proportion to the popularity of your contribution. Knowing how this works, the platform owners then have the option of realizing the financial worth of that content. In the process of doing so, they cleverly bypass you as the content creator. This is because you have unknowingly transferred the inherent value of your content to their platform.

Legally, you have to consent to this. This is why, when uploading content to a particular platform, you have to submit to an agreement that in legal terms counts as a contract. For the platform, this is a vital part of the process because they cannot legally acquire the rights to your content until you accede and agree to the terms stated in that contract. Consequently, the key issue for this contract is the crucial transfer of certain rights to the host platform.

This process does not just apply to music! When you express your thoughts and ideas on Facebook, you are contributing inherent value to that platform, which in this case is the value of your own words, thoughts and ideas. The value of Facebook then increases directly in proportion to your contribution. For the owners of Facebook at least, they now have the possibility to realize that value in financial terms. Value that has been provided completely for free by you, as the contributor and content creator.

Look at it another way.

For a professional author, thoughts and words comprise the vital content that enables them to earn a living. However, they can only earn this living when they a) understand the inherent value of their own thoughts and words and b) know how to use the mechanisms that allow them to realize that value in financial terms.

Put simply, if you want to retain the right to realize the financial value of any content that you create then you need to think twice before giving it away so easily.

VALUE AND RIGHTS

Having briefly explored the relationship between content and value, let us now see how rights enter into the picture.

The value that you bring to the world through your music can directly transform your life when you learn how to make use of the mechanisms that enable the conversion of that value into hard currency. These mechanisms all hinge upon the recognition of certain rights which the law recognizes that you automatically hold as the creator of that value.

In the world of music, there are two main rights with which you should be concerned. The first is intellectual copyright. This is your right to be identified as the owner of that music as a form of property, the right to make changes to it in any way that you see fit and the right to perform and play that music as part of a commercial

9

venture. 'Play' in this context, also means to transmit that music to the general public, whether through radio play, a jukebox, CD player, and so on.

The second is mechanical copyright. This is the right to make copies of an original recording reproduced in a particular format, whether this be in the form of CDs, vinyl, downloads, novelty gifts, and so on.

Your ability to earn a living from your music will all depend on what you do with those fundamental rights and the pathway that you pursue in order to be able to use those rights to your advantage.

One of the most common pathways people follow today is to transfer those rights to a publishing and/or record company, who will then exploit those rights commercially. In return for the transfer of those rights, the company will then pay you a cut (royalties) of all of the revenue that they generate through their exploitation.

Of course, how much money you can earn through this process is anybody's guess. And this is provided you can interest a company in the music that you create to begin with. Any interest that they do have will of course arise for only one reason - they believe they can make money from selling your music.

However, given the vastly oversaturated music marketplace today, even this recognised and well-travelled path can present certain problems. A friend of mine who is a well-known House DJ encountered such problems when he aspired to produce his own music. He spent a good few years developing and honing his music production skills to the point where he was ready to produce his first record.

Eventually producing his first release, he signed it with an independent record label and eagerly waited to see how his record would sell. At first it sold quite well, about forty or fifty copies over a fairly short period of time, but then sales of the record suddenly slumped. Looking in to the possible reasons for this, he discovered that his track was freely available for download on any number of pirate music sites.

Why would people go out and buy his record when they could simply download it for free?

With subsequent records the same pattern repeated itself, until he realized that it was almost pointless to even try to make a lot of money in this way. For every copy that was legitimately sold, there would be at least a hundred or so copies that were being illegally downloaded.

Another DJ also enjoyed a brief honeymoon period of sales with her first record, but found that sales soon dropped off. She felt that whilst the initial hype that her record label had created supported her early sales, the thousands of new releases, each with their own marketing strategy, soon drowned her release within a sea of noise.

It became apparent to both DJs that producing music in the form of MP3s to be sold to the general public was not necessarily the best way to earn money from their musical productions precisely because of these inherent vulnerabilities.

GET TO KNOW THE MARKETPLACE

Thankfully, the use of these mainstream channels is not the only way to earn money from writing music. There are other avenues that although potentially very lucrative, are less widely known. This is generally because they require a deeper knowledge of the music marketplace.

A good example are media production companies working in areas such as film, television, advertising, gaming and so on, whose business models largely depend upon being able to procure a steady supply of suitable music for their productions.

Any composer or music producer wishing to write music for a living would be wise to deepen their knowledge of these businesses. One approach would be to make a list of such media houses and having done so, examine how and in what way it might be possible to supply the music upon which they depend. In doing this you will discover that they all fall into one of two basic categories.

Firstly there are companies who depend upon the rights to be able to dub music onto a broadcast such as films, television programmes, advertisements, video productions and the like.

Secondly there are companies who rely upon being able

to copy and reproduce music within a particular format. Examples of this would be music that is used for apps, video and arcade games, novelty products such as birthday cards, children's toys and so on.

Observe that in the former case, the intellectual copyright is the most salient feature, whilst in the latter case it is the mechanical copyright.

WATCH OUT FOR NEW CHANNELS

Bear in mind that due to the continuing development of new technological capabilities, new and often unexplored channels for the commercial use of music are opening up all of the time.

If you keep abreast of these you may even be able to get involved in the development of an altogether new channel for the commercial use of music and in the process of doing so earn a lot of money. This happens more than one might realise, as can be seen when considering some examples of how this has already occurred.

The designers of early computer operating systems thought it would be a good idea to make them more user friendly with the use of some music, hence the Startup Sounds which every new computer user hears when they start up their computer.[2] At the time, this represented a completely new market for music, one

---

2 The History of Windows Startup Sounds, http://mashable.com/2012/10/24/windows-startup-sounds/#gallery/windows-startup-sounds/520c60645198406ae7000447

that most musicians might have ignored - after all, who wants to get involved in the creation of ditties?

However there is more to this than meets the eye. Even the most trivial seeming task can acquire a value directly in proportion to the degree of your input to it. In other words it is possible to take something that most people might ignore or trivialize and instead do the complete opposite and endow it with tremendous value.

Timing is an important feature of becoming involved in these emergent marketplaces. To confirm this we need only look at the history of the humble mobile phone ringtone. We have all heard stories about the rise of the mobile ringtone millionaires.

The most well-known is probably Alexander Amosu who went from writing and selling ringtones to sell to his friends for £1 each, to earning £1.6 million from the venture within the first year. On the way, this entailed opening up offices and employing some 21 people.[3]

Even a short book on how to customize your own ringtones sold more than 3½ million copies back in the day.[4] In fact, at one point, the mobile phone ringtone business was worth billions per year, and rivalled global digital music sales. All this from a marketplace that only opened up just over a decade or so ago.

---

3 Money Week, http://moneyweek.com/alexander-amosu-i-made-6-first-day-and-grew-from-there-44168/

4 Mobile Ringtones Do-Re-Mi Book, July, 1998.

Yet another example is music for video games. Like ringtones, this began with the innocuous use of sequences of electronic bleeps, noises and simple sine wave stings. They now reach a degree of distinction and sophistication that would have been unimaginable 10 or 15 years ago.

This is because each generation of composers who became involved with video game music chose to endow that music with a greater sense of value than had hitherto been given to it. In this sense, nothing in the world is ever set and fixed, but ever receptive and responsive to the influx of new value.

Consequently, it is now not uncommon for video game music to feature symphonic orchestrations that easily match Hollywood film scores, often ingeniously juxtaposed and combined with carefully considered world music sounds or indeed, high quality and stylistically aware electronic musical productions.

Of course, this does not happen without its pioneers, those who were willing to go that extra mile to improve the quality of the music.

A notable example is the Danish composer Troels Folmann (b. 1974), who in 2006 won a BAFTA award in the New Games category for the music he produced for Crystal Dynamic's Tomb Raider: Legend.

Using a deft combination of all three of the elements mentioned above (symphonic orchestrations, world music sounds and electronica) Folmann pioneered a technique which he refers to as 'micro-scoring', whereby music is triggered in response to wherever the player is in the game. Utilizing this technique led to a player-oriented soundtrack that more faithfully reflected what was happening in the game.[5]

In this sense, as we have just seen, musical challenges are whatever you choose to make of them. No matter how trivial a job requirement might appear, it is always possible to enrich it with an increased sense of value and in the process raise it into something very special. And in so doing, you may also earn some much-needed revenue from it along the way.

---

5 An interview with Folmann on this subject can be found on Gsoundtracks: A Video Game Music Website, http://www.gsoundtracks.com/interviews/folmann.htm

2: Production music

Production music is a perfect example of the rise in inherent value of something that had formerly seemed fairly inconsequential. Also known as stock music, library music, or mood music, this is music that has been specifically produced in order to be licensed for use in film, television, video and a host of other media productions.

A production music library is a company that has been specifically set up to sell production music to their clients, which are the producers of various media. There are many such libraries in the world, the business models and workings of which will be discussed in later on in this book.

Production music as we understand it today began life in the early 20th century as sheet music specially composed to be played live alongside silent movies in cinemas. Having undergone various stages of evolution since then, it has now become a relatively sophisticated musical art form. Indeed, modern production music can now be heard in most contemporary media productions, from cinema and television to online videos and advertisements. All genres of music and sound are catered for, from traditional classical music scores to modern electronica and Foley sound effects.

IMAGE PROBLEMS

Admittedly, due to its humble beginnings, production music has tended to suffer certain image problems. For a long time production music was regarded as second rate, often being derogatively referred to as 'elevator music' or 'muzak' due to the bland, light orchestral scores that permeated many shops, hotel lifts and airports during the middle part of the last century. Because of this, production music did not tend to attract serious attention.

Over the last twenty years or so however, all of this has changed. Production music is now receiving a complete image make-over, not only as a great way for composers to find a ready market for their music, but also as a type of music that is noted for its increasingly high production values.

This is no doubt largely due to the fact that it has begun to attract the attention of professional composers of the highest possible calibre, composers who - no matter what job they are given - will always choose to endow that job with a supreme sense of intrinsic value and worth.

THE DEMAND FOR PRODUCTION MUSIC

Although this means that the marketplace is now becoming more competitive, the client demand for production music seems to be increasing, meaning that there is always plenty of work to go around. Just think of the number of different television channels operating at present, many of which run continuously for 24 hours a day, 7 days a week.

All of these depend upon a supply of programmes and advertisements for which the use of some kind of music will be considered more or less essential. Consequently, for a bright, able and enterprising composer, production music offers incredible opportunities for earning good money creating music, often from the comfort of your own home studio.

In doing so, you will be providing the creators of media productions with something that is absolutely vital to them. Indeed, if you do it right, success is virtually guaranteed.

This is because it is generally much cheaper and quicker for media producers to purchase a license for the use of production music obtained from a dedicated production music library, than it is to commission music specifically from a composer or to use mainstream pop music.

THE NEED FOR PRODUCTION MUSIC

Media productions work to tight deadlines and even tighter budgets, so having music instantly available at a fixed cost is enormously helpful. Furthermore, there is often very little point commissioning a composer to write original music for a media production, simply because many such projects have very similar requirements, meaning that it is far more cost effective for a company to use generic library music already written for the purpose.

A good example of this is the plethora of nature programmes on TV where the main requirement is for an uplifting, pastoral style of music. Picture a scene where the camera pans across a broad country valley and then zooms in on a picturesque, tree-lined riverbank. All the while in the background, a full string orchestra is playing rich harmonies that make us think of the beauties of nature.

Why commission a composer to write new and original music for this type of scene? This would entail not only a cost which might eat deeply into their allocated budget, but it would also be to commission a genre of music that is already well-represented. In terms of economic decisions alone, the use of pre-composed production music to fulfill the programme's incidental musical requirements significantly drives down the costs involved.

This does not mean to say that television programme producers never commission original music; often they may have very specific musical requirements, which may not easily be met by a production music library. In these cases, although the cost will be significantly greater, the television producer will consider this a price well worth paying.

This often applies to the theme tune used for a programme. Needing to be a distinctive, memorable and unique feature of the programme, the producer will likely commission a composer to write an original theme tune that effectively conveys the identity and character of the programme. Any other incidental musical needs within the programme itself however, may be met by production music

PRE-COMPOSED PRODUCTION MUSIC

Like many other types of music, production music is created in studios specially equipped for that purpose. These can range from big-budget studios catering to large scale orchestral recordings, down to smaller and much more humble home studios. Indeed, due to the falling costs of the equipment required to produce professional quality recordings, there are now many musicians who successfully compose production music entirely within their own home studios.

For this general purpose, the use of both hardware and software synthesizers and samplers are of course invaluable items of equipment, together with the use of a suitable computer and appropriate software programs. Popular programs used for this very purpose are Pro Tools, Logic, Cubase, Ableton Live and Reason, to name but a few.

It is important to bear in mind that although production music in the past might have had a reputation for poor production values and musicality, this reputation is no longer justified. Indeed, you will find production music that achieves any degree of success in professional television and film productions usually has production values and a sense of musicality that is often as high as music released for the popular music market.

High-budget production music is still composed using live professional session musicians and orchestras, but these days savvy producers can emulate orchestral sounds using software for a fraction of the cost. Indeed, some composers of production music have so honed the art of using software to create orchestral sounds that it is often extremely difficult for the listener to determine whether or not real acoustic instruments are being used.

STYLES AND GENRES OF PRODUCTION MUSIC

However, not all production music will demand the use of a complete symphony orchestra. This is because production music uses a wide variety of different styles and genres, including modern popular music, electronic dance music, jazz, classical and so on. Inevitably, the instrumental forces used are those appropriate to the particular style or genre.

To get an idea of a range of different styles of contemporary production music, visit a production music site on the internet. Popular and well known libraries include Audio Network, Sonoton and Imagem. Once on the site the first thing you will notice is a menu that enables you to browse production music tracks according to various categories.

These enable the potential client to audition tracks according to their specific musical genre and style, the type of mood or emotion that they evoke, the instrumentation used in the tracks, the type of television programme that they might be suitable for and so on. Whilst browsing, you will see that a great number of different genres are represented. These are reflective of the fact that it is possible to use virtually any genre as production music.

Fig. 2: Some production music genres

This breadth of genre is beneficial to the production music composer, because for every type, style or genre of music they choose to produce, there will be a use for it somewhere in a production music library. Consequently the composer need never be limited by constraints upon the styles or genres of music that they are going to write, meaning that they can always remain within the range of those styles that they are most

25

comfortable and familiar with. But it also means that they can experiment with new styles should they wish. This gives the production music composer a great deal of freedom.

Having looked at what production music is and some of the ways in which it might be produced, let us now consider how you, as an interested party, might go about creating production music.

3: Creating Production Music

Generating a production music track generally takes place in three stages. We can appreciate what these stages are if we imagine the creation of production music at the most high-budget level, involving the use of a complete symphony orchestra.

The first stage of the process will be for a score to be produced by the composer. Although these scores used to be produced laboriously by hand, these days the job is made much easier by computer software.

A copy of the completed score is given to the conductor and the individual parts appropriately distributed to the orchestral players. Following rehearsal, the music will be recorded in a professional recording studio with engineers on hand to ensure that the recording meets a professional standard of studio and sound production. The music will then be mixed and mastered in order to create a high quality final master recording. Naturally, it is with this master recording that the interest of the production music library will lie.

The main point to understand from this model is that the creation of production music follows three basic stages. First the music is composed, then the music is produced and finally the music is mastered. Although these stages can be adapted to the particular type of music you are producing and the resources available to you, no matter what type of production music you produce it will inevitably have to go through these three stages.

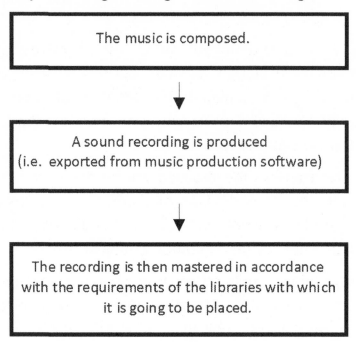

Fig. 3: *The three stages of creating production music.*

FLEXIBILITY OF RESOURCES

Very few production music composers will have access to the kinds of resources described in the foregoing example but this need not discourage you from writing orchestral production music if this is what you want to do. It simply means that it is necessary for you to be flexible and adaptable in terms of your approach and the resources that you use to do it.

Virtual orchestras - such as the Vienna Symphonic Library, the East-West/Quantum Leap Symphonic Orchestra or the Garritan Personal Orchestra for example - can now be used to create a very realistic orchestral sound. Using advanced sampling technology, one of the advantages of these virtual orchestras is that your written score can be played back in the comfort of your own home studio. Compared to the days when composers had to wait for rehearsals before they could first hear their score being realized, this is invaluable.

Effects such as reverb and a subtle delay can also be used to simulate the environments where orchestral recordings might occur, such as a large concert hall, an outdoor venue or perhaps even a cathedral, significantly enhancing the sense of the realism of the orchestral music.

Whether or not you need the resources of an orchestra hinges upon the types and styles of production music that you would like to create. Therefore although the use of a virtual orchestra is advantageous, it is by no means a necessity.

Because production music caters for all styles, genres and tastes, you need only obtain the resources needed for the particular styles of music that you will be writing. If jazz is your preferred genre, then you will be primarily working with instruments typically used in jazz ensembles. Of necessity, this represents an entirely different spread of instruments than would be required if you were working primarily with classical pastiche styles of music.

If on the other hand, your favoured genre is electronic music (which is also very popular in most production music libraries) you will be mainly using electronic instruments. These are well-catered for by software musical production programs such Logic and Reason. And where you would like to use acoustic instruments in your productions (pianos, strings or guitars as for example) realistic digital emulations of those traditional instruments are now very easy to obtain.

In effect this means that with even the most humble resources you can go on to compose, produce and even master your own production music, it is simply a matter of scaling your output to the resources that are currently available to you.

LISTEN TO PRODUCTION MUSIC

Before trying to write production music, you should first spend some time studying and familiarising yourself with the genre. For this purpose, it's a good idea to visit a number of high-ranking production music library websites and listen to their bestsellers. The website of the company Audio Network would be an ideal place to begin, since it is one of the largest and most popular libraries around.

In doing so, you will not only discover the kinds of production music that are particularly popular with clients, but you will also begin to see that production music has certain, readily identifiable character traits. These tend to derive from the fact that rather than be listened to as a musical work in its own right, production music is primarily functional because it has been created - or adapted - to be played alongside and as a part of various media. Being functional, production music therefore works within certain stylistic constraints that make it eminently usable for that purpose.

The most important constraints that you might identify are the length, theme and mood of individual music tracks. As these are important features of production music genres, let us now examine these three constraints and see how they affect and limit the process of composing and producing production music.

LENGTH OF TRACKS

Tracks that have been specifically composed as production music tend to be rather short. This is because it is extremely doubtful that a client is going to need the use of a long, extended and drawn out piece of music. You can understand the reason why by listening carefully to the way in which production music tends to be utilised in media productions. It is mostly used in short bursts that can even last for only a few seconds and it is very rare to find more than thirty seconds or so being employed at any one time.

An exception to this is music for television advertising, which may go on for a full minute or so. But by ordinary musical standards, even a minute is a very short time period. Suffice to say that, unless a client has specifically requested it, there is no point creating production music tracks that go on for longer than a few minutes. In fact, many pieces of perfectly good production music last little more than a minute in total length.

THEMES OF THE MUSIC

Because production music tracks might only be used for a few seconds at a time, they need to make their point clearly, quickly and as directly as possible.

Consequently, there is not a lot of point writing production music that features long winding intros. When that track is actually used in a television programme, the intro will simply be cut. If an intro is necessary for a track, it should always be as short and succinct as possible.

Another feature relevant to this is that many production music tracks tend to be monothematic. Although this sounds rather technical, it simply means that the track has been composed and built up from one readily identifiable theme. Giving the music a clear and obvious feel, groove or mood makes it eminently useable in a production music context.

Because of this, once a production music composer has created a strong main theme they will in effect have all of the essential material necessary to compose a complete production music track.

When composing a track, your first concern will be with the creation of the main theme.

THE MOOD OF TRACKS

Production music is generally used as a discreet audible background layer whose purpose is to help convey a certain mood, feel or atmosphere.

Because of this, a production music track whose music is bold and exciting will tend to build on this feeling throughout its entire length. With this in view, it is very rare to find production music that features drastic or notable contrasts of mood. The importance of this can be gauged by logging on to any production music library. Accessing the search engine, you will find that as well as genre, tracks may also be grouped by the particular mood they try to convey. As can be seen from Fig. 4, a wide range of different moods is catered for.

In Western music history, a strong precedent for this idea of 'mood music' was the concept of the Doctrine of the Affections which played such an important role in the aesthetics of the music and art of the Baroque period (around 1600 to 1750). The basic idea behind this was that a piece of music should ideally express just one particular mood or affection, whether this be love, hatred, desire, joy, sorrow or admiration. Composers who were strongly influenced by this idea thereby composed their music in order to reflect this expressive principle.

Fig. 4. *Examples of mood tags for production music*

PERTINENT QUESTIONS

In order to see how these principles apply to today's production music, it is worth spending some time listening to and studying the way in which production music is used on television programmes. As this is the way in which your own music will be used - if your tracks are accepted by a library – you should listen very carefully. While you are doing so, there are a number of pertinent questions that you could ask:

- How long was the music used for?

- How did the music complement the scene?

- What did the music bring to the scene?

- What general mood did the music suggest?

- What instrumental forces were being used?

- How did the music end?

Through doing this you will discover that television programme producers will often be very liberal when choosing suitable music. As long as the music conveys the particular mood, feel or atmosphere that is required, they will often use any type, style or genre of music that seems to be suitable. Because of this, production music libraries try to host music that runs the entire gamut of human feelings and emotions, thereby ensuring that every possible dramatic situation is being catered for.

Many production music composers therefore allow their creative choices to be led by the feel and mood that they are trying to put across. For the composer this represents a first class opportunity to have some fun putting together a range of sounds that they feel suitable for this purpose.

Canny production music composers will also try to anticipate what kinds of music are going to be needed in the near future. The clues for this will lie in whatever is currently happening in the world.

When the banking crisis occurred subsequent to the

crash of 2008, a lot of programmes were made exploring the causes of this crisis and the various issues involved. Production music clients therefore needed a plentiful supply of music that reflected the tense, edgy and fearful mindset prevalent at the time and savvy production composers were quick to meet the demand for tracks whose moods, themes and even titles reflected this particular ethos.

In simple terms, whatever is trending in the world at any given moment has the potential to become the subject matter for many media productions in the near future. By watching out for and studying these trends, you can create both work and opportunities for yourself by reflecting them in your production music output.

TITLES OF TRACKS

Although the title given to a track may not initially appear that important, it will often provide a powerful indicator of its general mood and feel. Bear in mind that the title will probably be the first point of contact that the client will have with a track. For this reason, when giving titles to your tracks, it makes sense to name them very carefully so that they provide a clear and unambiguous indication of what the client might expect. Even if your music ends up in a library that renames their tracks, a good title track will show the library your street smarts and help get your foot in the door.

Consequently, when trying to think of suitable titles for your tracks, try to look at your music from the standpoint of the client. A dark, edgy tune that you've called 'Sombre Horizon' may not attract as much attention as it would if it were named 'Streetlights and Shadows'. This is because the latter generates an immediate picture of night-time cityscapes in the mind of your client.

Also, be aware that your tracks will be listed alongside whole groups of such tracks. Because of this, it makes sense to give them catchy names that will help them to stand out and encourage the client to audition them. Alliteration, where the first consonant is repeated across multiple words (as in 'Streetlight Shadows') can sometimes be helpful here, provided it is not overdone.

Fundamentally, your choice of titles comes down to an understanding of consumer psychology, in this case the use of particular words and phrases that may capture the interest of a potential client. That interest may lead to the music being auditioned. Once auditioned it then stands a chance of being used by the library client. The title in this sense is an effective attractor of client interest.

4: Composing Production Music

Once you have gained a clear idea of what to expect from a production music track, you might then be tempted to try your hand writing your own production music. Generally speaking, you could go about this in one of two ways.

The first way is to try to write a piece of music that stands up entirely on its own as an example of mood music. The mood you choose to express does not matter at this stage; it will probably become clear to you as you work upon the track. The important feature in this approach is not so much what the mood actually is, but your ability to maintain and build upon it as you go.

The logic behind this is that if the music succinctly expresses a certain mood or feel, then it will work as a perfect musical background to media that requires that particular mood or feel.

Another much more specific approach is to imagine the hypothetical scene you are writing the music for in your mind's eye. Then try and create the music that you feel best belongs with it.

As you do so, some useful questions to ask would be:

- What general mood is required?
- What tempo would suit that particular mood?
- What instrumental forces would suit that particular situation?

If you find it difficult to imagine a scene in your mind, try bringing up a video on your computer and muting the sound. Then try to write some music that you feel would best go with a particular scene.

While doing so, bear in mind that the best production music tends to blend in so well with the scene that the audience may be hardly aware that music is even being played. In this context it simply provides a discreet audio background to the scene, one that suggests and implies certain emotions whilst making no direct or overt statements in itself.

Because of this, you might want to avoid writing flamboyant and tremendously technical instrumental solos that would tend to make the music more of a focal point than the visual scene itself.

KEEP IT SIMPLE

Another useful piece of advice is to keep the music as simple as possible. This can apply both to the forces that you use and the musical ideas upon which your track will be based.

Have you noticed how frequently a simple unobtrusive piano or guitar solo is used on television programmes? There is good reason for this. Simple solos can create a warmth and intimacy of expression that is suitable for a wide variety of production music uses and there is no reason to think that larger, more impressive forces are always better. As such, do not be afraid to keep the instrumental forces that you use as simple, direct and uncomplicated as possible. If one instrument can do the job, why use an entire orchestra?

An example of this can be found in Bob Dylan's 1963 hit 'Blowin' in the Wind' poses multiple questions over its three verses and then answers them rather ambiguously in the chorus. The instrumentation however is simply an acoustic guitar and harmonica.

Despite this economy of forces, this song is considered by many to be one of the greatest of all time and was inducted into the Grammy Hall Of Fame in 2004.

The same principle may be applied to musical ideas. The simpler and more direct those ideas, the more distinctive and memorable they will be. A straightforward, simple theme can often say a great deal more than a complex and intricate multilayered sound tapestry. To confirm this, think of your own experience of listening to television or film music. What springs to mind will probably be the music most notable for its use of simple, broad and expressive themes.

Less Is more

Another useful rule of thumb is that 'less is more'. Although seeming to embed a paradox, there is a great deal of wisdom in this rule. It indicates the two possible choices that can be made when composing production music. You can either do a little with a lot or a lot with a little.

Doing a little with a lot is wasteful; it is a far better practice to employ an economy of means. We can appreciate this by drawing a parallel with conversation. When somebody is trying to explain something to you but they keep going off at a tangent and introducing irrelevant elements, the experience can quickly become irksome because we recognize that a great deal of what they are saying is ancillary to the topic.

Compare that experience with listening to someone who expresses themselves with a series of clear, simple and lucid points, each of which contributes something valuable to the explanation. It is clear that in conversational terms, the first example shows someone doing a little with a lot while the second does a lot with a little.

Which do you prefer?

Exactly the same principle can apply to music.

Some of the greatest music that we are familiar with does a lot with a little. Consider the first movement of Beethoven's Fifth Symphony. We all recognize this movement due to its epic opening motif 'Da Da Da Daaaah'.

If you analyze this music you will discover that every single note of the movement has been somehow derived from that simple opening motif. The opening motif thus acts rather like a seed, from which the composer then grows an entire tree. In musical terms, this is a perfect example of doing a lot with a little. The result is an intense power of musical expression achieved by ensuring that no single note is actually redundant.

Another good example is John Williams' music for Stephen Spielberg's 1975 thriller 'Jaws'. When the shark is coming in for its attack, Williams uses a simple rising semitone motif which is then repeated at a progressively faster and faster tempo. This creates a feeling of escalating tension which perfectly complements the shark attack scenes, conveying the feeling of impending horror. The important point is that the musical material Williams uses for this is a simple motif made up from just two notes. The rest is simply repetition.

Equally, the 1965 hit '(I Can't Get No) Satisfaction' by the Rolling Stones is based on one simple, distinctive guitar riff that underpins both the verses and the chorus. This was a song that was deemed the 2nd best song of all time by Rolling Stone magazine.

In all three of these examples, complex themes with expressive power have been built from extremely simple motifs providing a perfect demonstration of the value of the rule: less is more.

CAUSE AND EFFECT

As a production music composer your job will be to use music as a means for evoking certain ideas, feelings and moods in your listener. Bearing this in mind, it's a good idea to start thinking about the ways in which the different parameters of music - the tempo, rhythm, melody, harmony, dynamics, instrumentation and so on - can be utilised towards this end.

To understand and make intelligent use of these parameters you will need to begin thinking about music in a different way for a while. Rather than regarding music as a vehicle of expression for your personal feelings, you will instead need to view it as a means for evoking feelings in your audience.

What, for example, what would be the most likely effect of a sequence of notes in a major scale whose pitch gradually rises? While the precise answer to this question will depend upon the specific context in which this occurs, a rise of pitch might generally be expected to produce feelings of hope, excitement and optimism. By contrast, a gradual fall of pitch might be expected to produce the opposite effect in the listener.

Another example is the use made of steps and leaps in melodic movement. Any melody is composed of only two types of melodic movement. There is movement by step, which proceeds from one scale degree to the next.

Then there is movement by leap where one or more scale steps is missed out. Here it is perhaps not surprising that a melody consisting of mostly stepwise motion will tend to produce a more calm and settled feeling than a melody that is full of erratic leaps. Consequently, if your intention is to create a feeling of agitation, the use of such irregular leaps might be a very effective way to evoke that mood.

USE OF MODES

One of the most effective means for conveying a particular mood or feel to an audience is through use of melodic modes. For the production music composer these modes offer an expressive resource comparable to the colours of an artist's palette. While a painter can create a certain mood and feel using colour, the production music composer can do the same through their use of mode.

Here it is no coincidence that the words 'mood' and 'mode' are very similar, and come from the same linguistic root. The connection between them goes back to ancient Greek music where every melodic mode was associated with its own particular ethos – that is to say, a certain atmosphere, colour or mood.

While the production music composer doesn't need to study ancient Greek modes and scales, they should at least be aware of the connection between mood and mode and the history that led to that connection. This is because modes represent an incredibly useful resource that can infuse their music with a vivid sense of colour and atmosphere.

This study may begin with the contrasting moods evoked by the major and minor scales of Western music, often termed the major and minor mode. The major mode for example, is well known for its ability to evoke a bright, optimistic and cheerful mood, especially when compared with the various modes of the minor scale.

The latter are clearly more suited to the expression of darker and more sombre feelings. One way to describe this would be to liken the major mode to the day and the minor mode to the night. Another useful comparison would be to compare the major mode with colours at the bright end and the minor mode with colours at the dark end of the solar spectrum.

To a degree much of this is entirely subjective, being largely based on audience associations and the resultant expectations that have grown up around them. Knowing what these are beforehand however allows you to use these to your advantage and thereby open up a valuable channel of communication with your prospective audience.

There are also more objective elements that have encouraged the association of particular scales with moods from the very beginnings of their use in music. These all hinge upon the tremendous expressive power of the musical interval - the difference or gap between two musical pitches.

It is no coincidence that in the major mode, the majority of the scale degrees bear a major interval relationship to the tonic (the primary note) while in the minor mode, the opposite is true. As each of these intervals contributes its own colour to the mode, the major mode with its major second, third, sixth and seventh tends towards the expression of bright, sunny emotions, and the minor mode, with its minor third, sixth and seventh tends towards the expression of darker and more serious feelings.

Whilst studying this subject, be sure to check out the subtle differences between the various minor modes. The natural minor mode for example can engender a beautiful, mellow mood, whilst the harmonic minor mode - with its augmented second inspired by Turkish music - has a fiery Eastern sense. The melodic minor mode in its ascending form meanwhile creates a sultry, smoky atmosphere, making it a favourite amongst jazz musicians.

The major and minor modes represent only a brief introduction to the subject of modes. There are literally hundreds of other musical modes that it is possible for a production music composer to use, each of which will have its own connotations in terms of the kinds of mood and atmosphere that they suggest.

Among these are the seven diatonic modes (Fig. 5)

which musicians still refer to using ancient Greek names, such as the Lydian, Aeolian, Dorian or Locrian mode. Each of these musical modes may be associated with particular moods, ranging from the lightness and joviality of the Lydian mode, the fierceness and austerity of the Phrygian mode and the stately power of the Mixolydian mode.

Fig. 5: The Seven Diatonic Modes (Key of C)

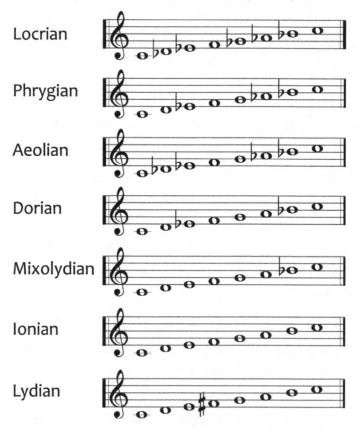

The subject of modes is well worth researching, because to know about them is to be armed with a powerful and extremely valuable tool for engendering certain feelings and moods in a receptive audience.

USING TONE COLOUR

Another vital agency for conveying mood and atmosphere is tone colour or timbre. This is the aural quality of the sound produced by each particular instrument and the means by which the ear most readily recognizes it.

The evocative power of tone colour can be easily demonstrated if we imagine a tune being played first on the flute and then on a trumpet. Although the melody might be the same, the mood will subtly change depending upon which of the two instruments it is being played upon. In the case of the flute, the mood will be lighter and more airy, while in the case of the trumpet the mood will be much more forthcoming and strident. Equally in electronic music, a Rhodes melody (as used in early Deep House) provides a far more delicate texture than the detuned sawtooths heard in Trance tracks of the same period.

Attention to tone colour particularly applies to the use of percussion instruments. Even though it is commonly assumed that the purpose of percussion instruments is to mark the beat, they have other more subtle, but equally vital uses as well.

When used sparingly in occasional touches throughout the course of a track, these colours can significantly contribute to the mood and atmosphere of a piece of music. For this reason, the production music composer would be well advised to spend time acquainting themselves further with this rich and diverse colouristic resource.

To understand tone colour properly it is necessary to begin exploring the connection between timbre and human emotion. This is a useful area of study for the production music composer - just a single note played on a particular instrument can be enough to begin evoking certain feelings and associations in the audience.

The sound of the oboe provides a perfect example of this. If you want to place the imagination of your audience into a rural scene, the oboe will do it. Played in legato style it can speak of relaxing in the great outdoors, while played staccato, the rustic mood can suddenly become more raucous and playful.

The harp provides another good example. Used in one context, it can take your listener into the dark, mysterious depths of the ocean, whilst used in another it can just as easily suggest the ethereality of outer space, particularly when the delicate, bell-like harmonics of the instrument are being played.

A study of instrumentation - a classical compositional discipline – can also benefit the composer of production music. If you like to use strings for example, check out the different ways in which stringed instruments can be bowed.

Bowed with the bow near the bridge, instruments such as violin or viola can produce an ethereal, whispering kind of sound, whilst bowed over the fingerboard, a soft, dreamy, floating type of sound results.

Similarly, when the strings are plucked with the fingers rather than played with the bow, the tongue-in cheek sound of pizzicato is obtained, a great favourite with production music composers.

Admittedly, some of these techniques might have now become clichés in production music circles – especially the use of pizzicato strings. But as these clichés are now embedded in the mind and psychology of your audience, it makes a great deal of sense to find out what they are, why they work and how to use them to your advantage.

WORLD MUSIC SOUNDS

There are an enormous variety of instruments used in world music that are perfect for producing a sound characteristic of the place from which they originate. There is nothing like the use of a particular national instrument to evoke powerful associations with a particular country or part of the world.

To appreciate this, picture Taoist monks meditating in their caves in the Western mountains of China.

If asked to think of a musical instrument that could

quickly evoke the sense and atmosphere of this, it is very likely that the sound of the bamboo flute would come to mind. This is all a part and parcel of the extraordinary power of tone colour to summon the atmosphere of exotic places and spaces.

Other obvious examples of this are the association of pan pipes with the mountains of Peru, singing bowls with the Buddhist monks of Tibet, the balalaika with the sound of Russia, bamboo pipes with the Far East, the Spanish guitar with Flamenco music, the oud with the music of the Middle East, the sound of the koto with Japan and the sitar with India.

Through discreet use of tone colours that draw upon these powerful associations, the thoughtful production music composer can suggest virtually any environment or location upon the planet to the receptive listener. Whilst it is wise to avoid overused and obvious clichés – such as male voice choirs to suggest Wales - the subtle use of world music instruments and sounds still represent an important source of expressive tools and techniques for the production music composer.[6]

---

6 Check out MIMO, the Music Instruments Museums Online which has one of the most extensive online databases of world music instruments.

5: Production Values

One of the challenges of creating production music is that as well as composing the music, you will also need to produce it as well. As these are different tasks - each requiring a different skillset, let us now consider some of the essential differences between them.

When composing production music, you will be trying to create a perfect example of the particular genre that your music might represent. Therefore, if your composition project is for solo piano for example, the intention will then be to compose such a superb example of this genre, that every library you send the composition to will want to snap it up.

The challenge of producing however is to create a sound recording (or a virtual simulation of one) that enables your composition to be heard at its absolute best. This is a completely different skill from composing in the sense that it is much more practical, hands on and very much more technical in the demands it puts upon the production music creator.

The difference between composition and production can be better understood when we look at some of the outcomes that are possible when the two tasks have been completed.

You could compose a wonderful piano solo that no production music library actually wants, because it is being let down by poor production standards. In this case, a fine composition is then being let down by a bad sound recording.

There are many possible reasons for this. The tone of the piano you used might sound just too weak and tinny, or perhaps too much reverb has been applied, causing the music to sound like it has been recorded in a massive, empty room.

Alternatively, you could create an absolutely splendid sound recording, but no library wants it because it is being let down by the poor quality of the composition itself - in other words a mediocre composition is being propped up by a fine sound recording. Again there are various possible reasons for this. It could be that a modulation in the music sounds too sudden and abrupt, or perhaps the melody line itself sounds rather weak.

Naturally, as neither of these extremes is desirable, the aim will always be to create an inspired musical composition that is then complemented by an expertly produced sound recording.

OVERLAPS BETWEEN COMPOSITION AND PRODUCTION

Although composing and producing are different tasks,

in actual practice they will frequently overlap with one another. When creating a production music track you will often find yourself alternating between them.

A good example of this is the process of creating a drum track for your project. Having composed a kick-snare pattern that you like, rather than composing anything else (such as a hi-hat pattern), you may then decide to spend some time improving the sound quality of the drum samples you have used. For example, you might not be happy with the sound of your snare drum sample. You may decide either to tweak it, or replace it with a more suitable sample. Note that this latter task is an issue of music production, rather than music composition.

Having seen to this, you might only then decide to return to the process of composition i.e. composing the particular hi-hat pattern that you would like to use. After composing and sequencing a suitable pattern, you may then return to the process of production, by trying to get exactly the right kind of sound for your hi-hats.

Therefore because processes of musical composition can often alternate, intermix and combine with processes of musical production, do not assume that it is necessary to compose a track in its entirety, before then going on to produce it, since it rarely turns out that way in reality.

However, as producing your tracks is a job that is equally as important as composing them, let us now consider some of the main skills that you are going to need as a production music producer.

Naturally, as this is a vast subject, in this particular chapter we will tend to focus upon some of the more obvious pitfalls and traps that it is possible to fall into and how best to avoid them. They assume that you already have the use of a suitable music studio, even if that only be your own home studio setup.

PROJECT FOLDERS

One of the biggest potential traps is a lack of essential preparations for a production music project. Production music often tends to be produced in clusters or groups of related tracks. Depending upon the specific job requirement, these groups of tracks might reflect an over-riding theme such as nature, ancient history or industrialization for example.

Whatever the theme is, the tracks that you create for this project will need to reflect that theme in some way. A good example of this is illustrated in fig. 6. which shows a set of audio files within one subfolder of a themed project. This particular project consisted of thirty-two tracks in twenty-six separate folders which were then stored in one main folder. Involving a total of 832 separate audio files, the necessity for organizing one's work properly could not be made more clear.

Fig. 6: Audio files belonging to a subfolder of a production music project.

Even with no overarching theme to govern your production, you will still tend to create production music tracks in related groups. This is because once you really get going, the creation of a single track won't take you that long – especially if you feel inspired. For this reason you could be composing a considerable number of tracks within a fairly short time period. You are therefore going to need to store these tracks in a folder containing all of the relevant files belonging to that project.

The importance of this organized method of working will become even more apparent when we come to cut-downs, in which each production music track will be represented in up to six or seven forms, each with its own particular length. As such - given that your project might consist of a dozen or so different tracks - you could in total be storing perhaps 144 separate tracks in a particular folder.

For this reason, you always need to be very organized about your work and make sure that everything is neatly stored in folders that are then appropriately backed up either on an external device or cloud storage.

INITIAL SETTINGS

Once your folder has been set up, you can then begin working on the individual projects that will be stored therein. Here there are a number of potential pitfalls that need to be avoided. One such lies in the initial settings for the recording of the track.

For each of these individual projects it is vital to set the parameters of your sequencer in such a way as to facilitate the recording and editing of the music.

The most important initial parameters are the tempo and the time signature. There is nothing worse than recording a track in the wrong tempo or wrong time signature. Everyone has done this at some time or another and always deeply regretted it afterwards. This is because it makes it virtually impossible to edit the track or divide it up into suitable lengths for cut downs.

If you fail to set the tempo so that each bar of music in real time corresponds to a single bar on your sequencer, then when the time comes to edit, copy, paste or break the track down into smaller cuts, you won't know where to begin or end. The result will be a feeling of acute frustration and much time being wasted.

It is therefore sensible to spend some time establishing the ideal tempo for the track right at the start and then set the sequencer to that tempo. Once the track has been recorded at this tempo, it can then be speeded up or slowed down as need be. The important point is that you know the ideal tempo at which to properly record the music. You will know this because bar sixteen of your music in real time will correspond with bar sixteen of your sequencer.

The next issue to address is your sequencer's time signature setting. Although getting this setting right becomes less important once the tempo has been decided, it can still be frustrating if for example, your sequencer window is divided into 4/4 measures, while your track is actually in 12/8 time.

This will mean that each bar of the music in real time will take up one and a half bars in your sequencer window, which in turn will give you problems identifying where the bars actually begin and end. You will find this tremendously frustrating when you subsequently need to cut the track down into convenient lengths.

In this particular instance, you would have two choices. You could either set the sequencer to a time signature of 4/4 and use a note resolution of one-eight triplets (1/8T) or else you could set your time signature to 12/8 – which is probably the easiest option.

Having set the time signature, remember that if the time signature of the music changes at any point you will then need to go in and program those corresponding changes of time signature into your sequencer.

The overall aim is to have your sequencer faithfully reflect both the tempo and time signature of your music when performed and played in real time. This way, when you go on to edit the music, the entire process will be easy, convenient and much quicker.

Naming Individual Sequencer Tracks

Once you have set up suitable settings for your project you can then begin to think about the recording process. For this purpose you will be recording the music on a number of separate sequencer tracks which will then appear in the project window of your chosen sequencer.

While doing so, bear in mind that this will be just the beginning of the process. In this respect, it will be similar to the first draft of an essay. The main ideas will be laid down but it will not yet count as an edited and polished final product. Inevitably, the number of sequencer tracks that you use will depend upon the project itself. A simple piano solo might use a single track, whilst a complex multi-timbral orchestral project might use over a hundred or more tracks.

Thankfully, modern software programs often cater very well for the use of a large number of sequencer tracks and provided that your computer's CPU can cope with this, feel free to use as many tracks as you deem necessary.

You can save yourself a great deal of frustration if you give each sequencer track a readily identifiable name. Although less critical when working with relatively few tracks, the importance of naming them rises incrementally with the number of tracks that you use. If you use a large number and don't name them, you will inevitably end up wasting a lot of time searching for a particular track. When they are properly named however, they become much quicker to identify and locate.

Some producers also like to use colour to back up the name. If you always colour the track label of your main drums with the colour red for example, you will then be able to find your drum track at a glance, often without even referring to the name you have given it.

RECORD TRACKS FROM THE BOTTOM UP

When recording your projects, there is never just one way to do it and it is therefore rather pointless to discuss the recording process using terms such as 'should' and 'shouldn't'. Each producer has to find their own way of working, using whatever knowledge they have managed to acquire and learn along the way.

Having said that, there are easier and more difficult ways to record production musical projects. For example, it is generally easiest to record a project from the foundations up. In practical terms this means first of all laying down the percussion track and any bass that might be used. In some ways, this is rather like building a house upon solid foundations. Once the foundations have been put in place they offer a firm support the upper parts such as the walls and the roof.

In terms of production music, the foundation for the rhythm is often provided by the drum track. As such, if your project does use drums, lay that track down first of all, if only for as many bars as you need to get the project underway.

This will then help you enormously with the timing when you lay down any of the other tracks i.e. the bass, lead melody, fills and so on. Few producers like to work with a click track if they don't have to and laying down the drum track first obviates any need for this.

Next, if you can and the project allows for it, lay down the bassline. This will then give your track the much needed acoustic foundation upon which all of the other tracks will then rest. These may include tracks for your lead melody together with any fills such as arpeggios, chord stabs, and so on.

It is of course feasible to begin the recording process by laying down the melody line first. However, this can be akin to building a house from the roof downwards. Consequently, while it may occasionally work, the extra time required might compound and eventually adversely affect your working speed in the long term.

As we have said, there is no absolutely definitive way to

lay a production music project down. And as soon as attempts are made to try to assert one, an exception will then be found that renders it useless for that particular type of project. As such it is always necessary to be supremely flexible and adapt one's methods to the needs of the track and the resources being used. The bottom upwards approach should therefore only be applied to those projects for which it proves itself to be suitable.

QUANTIZATION

Quantization is and can be a tricky issue when it comes to producing production music. Quantization is the automatic alignment of musical events according to the terms of a particular note resolution. Therefore, if the note resolution of your sequencer quantizing function is set to, for example, one-sixteenth note, when applied every note of the track will then begin precisely at the start of each sixteenth.

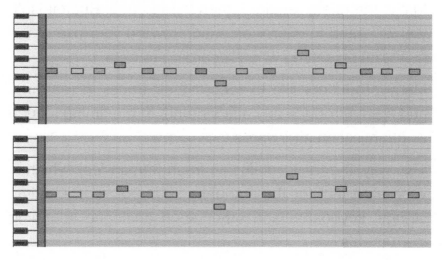

Fig. 7. *Unquantized and quantized bass pattern*

This process is illustrated in fig. 7. In the upper window a one bar bass pattern appears as it was crudely recorded, meaning that it is unquantized. Observe that some of the notes come in a bit earlier than required, others slightly later. In the lower window the bassline pattern has now been quantized. Here you can see that all of the notes now begin precisely at the start of each sixteenth note – as indicated by the grid.

It is also possible to record one's MIDI input with the quantization setting on. This means that despite any subtle deviations in one's timing as the notes are being played in and recorded, each note of the track will be automatically shifted so that it will begin on say, the nearest sixteenth note.

Although it might be tempting to record with the quantization setting on, one such consequence of this is that it may lead to the track sounding too mechanical. If that is the effect required, then fair enough. But if it isn't, you will need to exercise caution toward your use of the quantization setting when recording tracks.

Many producers like to record their tracks in real time and then introduce any adjustments to the timing – such as quantization afterwards.

This way, the track retains its fresh human feel, which is very important for the authentic sound of vocals, guitar, strings, keyboards and other such analogue sounding instruments.

Thankfully, quantization can usually be set to a certain percentage of the required note resolution. This is beneficial because it can help counter the tendency of over-quantized music to sound too robotic. Most contemporary sequencers also provide quantization settings that have been specifically devised in order to tighten the rhythm, but retain the natural, human feel of the track.

EDITING INDIVIDUAL TRACKS

Once a track has been recorded onto the sequencer, it can then be edited to one's own satisfaction. Here, any evident mistakes can be corrected and sorted out. This can include processes such as correcting the pitch of wrong notes, adjusting the position of certain notes in the bar or perhaps lengthening notes that go on for too long. Here there are a number of potential pitfalls which the production music composer should be aware of.

The first is a temptation to overwork the editing of the track. The need to do this might be due to a mistaken belief that the more one edits it the more perfect the track will sound. Editing however is not some kind of philosopher's stone. It cannot turn dull lead into bright, shining gold. All it can do is allow you to remedy obvious defects.

There is a cautionary tale of one composer who - having been asked to produce a theme tune for a television series - went in to the studio and quickly recorded some initial ideas. One idea in particular really stood out, so he opted to work on that.

Having originally created a rough, five minute take, he then set about editing the music to make it sound more polished and professional. He spent weeks doing this, but the results of each attempt left him with the feeling that the music had lost a certain vital something and attempting to regain that magic he would edit the track some more. Each time however this made the track sound worse rather than better.

Frustrated, he contacted the programme producer to let him decide which of the many takes he would prefer to use. After listening through all these different edits, the producer went on to choose the first ever take that had been knocked out in just a few minutes!

The upshot is that the composer had just wasted a couple of months trying to perfect something that due to its sheer sense of ease, freshness and spontaneity, was already a gem as shiny and perfect as it could be.

Another potential pitfall is the temptation to begin editing the music too early. I know many music producers who have great difficulty finishing their projects. This is because they spend so much time fussing over the minor details of individual tracks that by the time they get to laying down another track, they have lost all sense of their original idea.

In order to avoid this, do not worry too much about getting every individual track sounding perfect from the very beginning. If some notes come in slightly too early or perhaps a touch late, just leave them be for now. First of all, get a rough sketch of the whole project laid down before going in to edit individual tracks in detail.

Also be careful to save each run of edits as a separate file. That way, if you do make a mistake or want to return to the freshness of your original sketch, you can do without any trouble.

EDITING NOTE DATA

Sequencer tracks record many essential types of data, all of which can be satisfactorily edited.

Note data informs your sound producing instrument what notes to play, how loud to play them, for how long and when to play them. When you play a wrong note and go into the piano roll view of your sequencer to correct it, you are in effect making an adjustment to this particular type of data. The parameters with which you will mainly be concerned will be the pitch, duration and timing of the notes that have been recorded onto a particular sequencer track.

All of this information will be presented to you visually in the piano roll of the individual sequencer track upon which the recording has taken place. This allows you to play back your recorded track and as you do, watch the piano roll. Any errors or points where changes can be made can be spotted and noted down for editing either immediately or later on.

The most common errors are wrong notes which can be corrected as required by adjusting their pitch up or down in increments of semitones. Editing the duration of notes is also a routine procedure. If a note is too short in length it can be lengthened by the necessary amount; if it goes on for too long it can be shortened.

Edits can also be productively made to the timing of the notes. When recording a track in real time it is common for certain notes to come in slightly too late or early. Fortunately, the position of these notes in the bar can be flexibly altered on the piano roll, so that they then enter at the right time.

When you are judging what that right time actually is, try not to be a slave to the sequencer grid. If a note does not fall exactly in line with the grid this does not necessarily mean that its timing is therefore wrong. It simply means that it is not in alignment with robotic time. Try to use your ear to judge the time. If the note sounds like it is coming in at the right time, then leave it be, whatever its position relative to the sequencer grid!

EDITING NOTE VELOCITY

As velocity is the relative level of volume of the notes that are played on a particular channel or track, notes that have been played too loud or soft can be edited by changing their velocity. If a note is too loud in the track its velocity can be lowered, while if it is too quiet the velocity can be raised.

This can also apply to groups of notes. Sometimes a note group could benefit from having their velocities raised or lowered by a certain amount. When dealing with note groups the phenomenon of velocity curves starts to become more important.

Ideally, a good velocity curve would reflect the way in which a musician might naturally play a given sequence of notes. For example, they might put a slight emphasis on some notes while playing others more lightly. Thankfully, the velocity curve can be adjusted by raising or lowering the velocities of individual notes by the required amount.

EDITING CONTROL DATA

Another important type of editable data is control data, which creates a record of the precise settings (and any changes made to those settings) of the various controls used upon your sound producing device. Examples of these are output level, pitch bend, portamento, low frequency oscillation rate, filter frequency and so on. If a controller (knob or slider) exists on a given device, there will be a control data channel provided for it on your sequencer.

In accordance with globally standardized MIDI protocols, each type of data will carry a particular number from 0 – 127. This number will enable you to identify the data type and thereby locate the control data channel where that data will then be recorded and stored. For example, the volume control will carry the number 07, panning the number 10, sustain pedal the number 64 and so on.

Although remembering what these numbers refer to is not important at this stage, it is useful to know that this data will be recorded on those designated channels. Because of this, you can then makes changes to this data in the same way that you can edit note data.

If, for example, you notice in bar twenty-seven of your project that the sustain pedal cut-off is coming in too late, you can edit the sustain pedal data to correct it. In this sense, the different types of note data coupled with various channels of control data give you complete determination and control over every possible parameter of your project.

Sound effect

Another common temptation for the would be production composer is to try to enhance the sense of atmosphere and appeal of their music through use of sound FX. A clichéd example of this would be to introduce the sounds of creaking doors, clanking chains and hooting owls in a horror themed musical project!

Although this might be tempting, bear in mind that the adding of Foley sound effect to a television programme is a separate job from music synchronization and it is carried out by trained experts. As such, any sound effect that you have added might conflict with the Foley artists' range of sounds used within a scene. Basically this would mean that your music would then be unusable.

Because of this, try instead to develop your skill as a music composer to convey atmosphere. It is after all, this particular skill that a library will be looking for.

6: Mixing and mastering

As production music producer you will be learning and practicing four main skills. These are the skills of recording, editing, mixing and mastering of your music. While the skills of recording and editing tend to focus more upon the content of individual tracks or sequencer channels, the skills of mixing and mastering tend to focus more upon the way all of those channels sound when played together.

For example, when you are mixing a track you will be primarily concerned with the way in which individual tracks sit in the mixdown of the project as a whole. As such, the process of mixing will mainly rely upon the use of an information feedback loop between the master outputs (that enable the mix to be monitored) and the individual outputs of particular tracks.

Your job is therefore to monitor that information and where necessary, make those adjustments necessary to create a perfectly balanced mix. Bearing this in mind, let us now consider the outgoing and return flows of information that belong to this feedback loop. As proceeding in one direction (master output to individual track) the flow of information will be from the general to the particular. This is based upon your monitoring of the sound of a given sequencer track as a part of the overall mix, and the assessment and detection of any changes that then need to be made to that individual track.

A simple example of this is the volume of a particular track. If a given track stands out too much in the mix, the volume slider of that individual track will then need to be adjusted until the level sounds just right.

As proceeding in the other direction (individual track to master output) the flow of information is then from the individual to the general. How have these changes made to that individual track impacted upon the mixdown of the track as a whole? Is the volume level of that track now better? Has this change of level adversely affected the overall balance of the mix? If so, how can this be remedied?

Mixing is therefore a cycling process that is dependent upon your monitoring of the flow of information in both of these directions. For this reason when you are mixing, you will always be fluctuating between the standpoints provided for by the two poles involved in this process – the individual and master output tracks.

While mixing, it's also worth thinking about the intended medium of your music. Dance music can often be bass-heavy, but production music is often played on televisions, laptops and tablets – media that don't reproduce bass well. That's not to say that you shouldn't harness the power of bass for when your music is played on a big surround sound system, but you'll notice that production music tracks have a certain sheen in the upper frequency registers, just like tracks intended for mainstream radio airplay – you'd do well to harness this.

INSERT AND AUXILIARY EFFECT

The cycle of adjusting and monitoring is nowhere more clearly represented than in the difference between insert and auxiliary effect. Consequently, to be able to mix your music properly, you will need to know the essential difference between insert and auxiliary effect, as well as the range and type of effects that it is possible to use in both of these contexts.

Inevitably, this knowledge can only be gained through direct experience of hands-on experimentation with different types of effects, discovering how they can be used to affect the overall sound. Suffice to say, reading about reverb or chorus will not be sufficient in its own right. You need to be able to hear it for yourself, especially the ways in which a given effect might be adjusted in order to get the effect required.

Naturally, the more time that you can put into this, the better the results you will then achieve.

Insert effects are those applied to individual channels of the mix and thereby exert an effect only upon those particular channels. Auxiliary effects by contrast, are those applied to the final master outputs, meaning that they have the potential to exert an effect upon every single channel that requires them. This is done through the auxiliary sends on your mixer.

It is extremely important to understand not only the differences between these two types of effects, but also their individual roles when contributing to the mix as a whole.

INSERT EFFECT

In so far as insert effects are concerned, there are two main axioms that tend to govern their use.

The first is that insert effects provide you with a roster of sound processing tools that can help you to create the right quality of sound that you require for a given track. In this context, your own aural imagination will often provide you with the best guide as to which effects to use.

It is important that you try to match the sound that your sequencer track is producing as closely as possible with the sound that you can hear in your aural imagination. Inevitably, this can entail a lot of experimentation in terms of what it is possible to do with insert effects.

You may for example find that surreptitious use of a phaser on a given track produces the very sound that you are looking for. In this case therefore, you will be using the phaser as an expressive sound modulator. Alternatively, you might find that your subtle use of reverb brings a virtual orchestral instrument or acoustic guitar track to life.

The important point is that without the use of insert effects, the sounds being produced by your sequencer will often count as being no more than raw material.

The second axiom is that your use of insert effects will be governed by your need to produce the quality of sound an experienced listener might expect from a track of that kind. In this case, the effects will primarily be used as sound processors whose purpose is to shape and perfect that sound in accordance with a listener's expectations.

An obvious example of this is the use of reverb and delay on a guitar in a dub reggae track. As the use of this type of effect is integral to the sound of that type of guitar line, its absence would thereby represent a failing on the part of the producer to fulfill that expectation.

At this level, it is your own standpoint as an experienced listener, together with a growing knowledge of the use and application of insert effects that will provide you with the best guide as to the type of effects to be used.

AUXILIARY EFFECT

Auxiliary effects are those applied to the auxiliary channels of the mix. They won't have an effect on the mix until a signal is sent from a mixer track to the auxiliary channels. This signal is sent by using the auxiliary sends on the mixer. They are thus capable of exerting an effect upon none, some, or each and every channel of the mix.

There are some great advantages to this. If for example you want a particular type of reverb on numerous tracks, rather than attaching a separate reverb device to every channel of the track and then duplicating its settings, you can simply set reverb up as an auxiliary effect.

It is important that your use of auxiliary effect is in harmony with your use of insert effect. For example, when applying reverb to a strings patch, you could decide to use a hall reverb as an insert effect upon that channel. However, given the probability that you might want to use that very same reverb as an auxiliary effect, you may want to check whether it is actually necessary to give that particular channel its own reverb. Instead you could use the auxiliary send on that channel to create an equivalent effect.

The same consideration might apply to the use of stereo chorus effect. This is great for obtaining a richer, thicker sound from string patches - but you may need it on other channels of the mix as well. In this situation you will need to determine whether stereo chorus is better utilised as an insert or auxiliary effect. Ultimately, such decisions can only be made by considering the needs of the mixdown as a whole.

PANNING AND THE STEREO FIELD

When writing a piece of production music, you are creating a product which will at some point be received and heard by a listener. While producing your music it will help enormously if you try to put yourself into the position of that listener. How will your music be experienced by the

One of the important parameters that relates to the listener's experience of music is the stereo field. Representing an arc that sweeps from left to right with the listener themselves at dead centre, panning concerns the position from which a sound is heard to come relative to that stereo field. In other words, the signal coming from a channel that has been panned to the left will be perceived by the listener to be coming from the left hand side of the stereo field and vice-versa.

Setting the respective panning of each channel of your mix is therefore an important part of the mixing process. Towards this end, bear in mind that when a channel is given its own unique position in the stereo field, it then occupies its own discrete space within that field. This in turn makes it easier for the listener to distinguish it from the sounds coming from the other channels.

The way in which real life instruments would be located on stage relative to an audience represents one of the best guides to panning.

However, there is also a creative element involved, whereby interesting and novel effects can sometimes be achieved through thoughtful experimentation with these parameters. A good example of this is the effect of stereo cross-panning, wherein the signal from the left channel gradually moves over to the right as the signal from the right channel simultaneously shifts over to the left.

You should be cautious not to over-pan the primary instruments of your mix – as a guide, keep them between roughly three o'clock and nine o'clock on the pan pot.

REVERB

Reverberation occurs when sound waves hit the surface of a material and rather than being absorbed, bounce back off it, rather like a ball thrown at a wall. It is through our perception of reverberation that we acquire a sense of the space in which the sound is occurring. Hence if all reverberation is removed from a recording the sound becomes very flat and it loses a lot of its life. This is because, in reverberating, the sounds are carrying information about the precise nature of that space – information which our ear is easily capable of detecting.

Reverb effects are those hardware or software devices that have been created in order to specifically simulate the reverberation properties of various spaces. The intelligent and thoughtful use of these devices is an essential feature of any good mix, particularly when the sources of sound that we are using are primarily synthetic, since we will then have to apply reverb as an insert effect in order to give those sounds a sense of depth, presence and realism.

When applying reverb we need to ask ourselves what kind of space we want to put our listener into. Is it a space that is enclosed? If so, is that space a small room, a hall or a huge stadium? Or are they perhaps in a more open space such as a park, on top of a mountain or in the midst of a dense forest? Suffice to say, reverb is an essential concern when one is mixing down a track, especially if we want our track to sound realistic and authentic.

Whilst I won't delve into the various techniques used to simulate reverberation, it is worth noting that different reverb machines (or plugins) use different algorithms to simulate reverberation. These algorithms all possess a different character. Any aspiring producer would be wise to research different reverb units to find one that suits their sound, rather than use the first one they come across.

LEVELS

Volume levels are one of the most important aspects of the mixing process. First, consider the level of each individual track. This needs to be just right for the mix as a whole. Here the primary consideration is with the clarity and depth of sound of a particular channel.

- Ask yourself whether it sits just right in the mix?

- Is the sound of that particular channel clearly audible?

- Is it too quiet or perhaps too prominent?

Naturally when trying to answer these questions a great deal of experimentation will need to take place during which levels will be constantly adjusted and revised until the mix sounds just right to your ear. Again, the main guide here will be your own aural imagination.

- Does the mix tally with your imaginative vision of it?

- If not, what needs to be done to adjust it?

Secondly, the level of the mix as a whole will need to be reviewed. Here you will be concerned with the level of the signal coming from the master outputs. A common mistake that can be made with this is to think that 'loud is better'. On the contrary, for production music, balance is always better, not the sheer level of volume.

In terms of the level of sound signals coming from the master outputs, you are aiming for a level that is always below the maximum output of 0 decibels. This is because you need to leave sufficient room for the mastering process. Whether the mastering service is provided by the library or you master the track yourself, it is during the mastering that the final level will then be set. Whilst mixing therefore, aim for a level somewhere between 3 dB and 6 dB below the 0 dB maximum, in other words an output of -6dB to -3dB.

It is also important that you never try to use fade-out in order to bring a track to an end. Although it might be tempting to introduce a fade at the end of your piece - especially when you can't think of a clear ending - fade-out is not an appropriate part of the production music genre. Production music needs to begin and end clearly and concisely. This is because it has to be properly synchronized and that synchronization process is often matched to the nearest second.

MASTERING

Mastering is one of the most problematic tasks that a production music producer will probably encounter. This is because mastering is essentially a matter for trained experts in the field. For music to be properly mastered to broadcast quality it is often sent to mastering engineers who know exactly what they are doing.

As such, when producing music for a particular library or media company, always enquire as to their policy concerning mastering. Libraries and media companies often prefer to take care of the mastering so that it can then be accomplished in accordance with their own exacting and often very rigorous requirements.

When this applies, your responsibility as a production music producer will then be to provide them with no more than a balanced mixdown that that can then be mastered without any problems.

If the responsibility for mastering the music lies with you, only proceed if you consider yourself to be an expert in the field. If this is not the case, it could be a worthwhile investment to send your music to a professional to be properly mastered since doing so might make all the difference between having your track accepted or rejected by a music library. Online services like LANDR are also available if you can't afford a professional, and whilst their automated processes lack the nuanced ear and personal touch of a professional mastering engineer, they can suffice as a quick and dirty method of mastering tracks intended for demo use.

7: Cut-downs

Having looked at the art of composing and producing production music, let us now consider the process of creating cut-downs. Every production music composer needs to learn how to do this and to then practice this art to the point that it becomes second nature. Thankfully, it is not necessary to create cut-downs for every production music track that we write; only those tracks that the library has agreed to take will need to be cut down.

Cut-downs are where a production music track is broken down into a series of usable lengths of different, standardized durations. These are designed so that the piece of production music can fit neatly into media of different standard durations, such as a 30 or 60 second television advertisement for example.

An illustration of a piece of production music with these standardized cut-downs is shown in fig. 8. Observe that the track as a whole is 2 minutes and 28 seconds in length.

Below it a series of standardized cut-down lengths are shown, the longest of which is one minute. This is followed by the thirty second cut-down and subsequent cut-downs of 15, 10 and 5 seconds respectively.

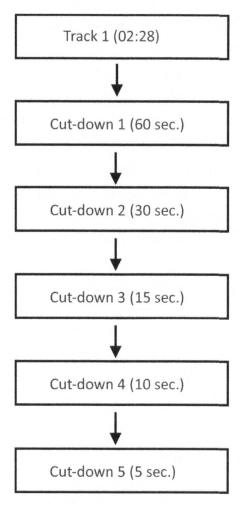

Fig. 8: *An example of the range of cut-downs that would be made from an original piece of music*

On occasion, a 20 second cut-down may be required in place of the 15 second cut-down. Because of this, enquire from the library placing your tracks for the exact length of the cut-downs that they prefer.

Creating cut-downs is one of the most technically demanding tasks in writing production music. It can also be very frustrating, because as you hack your tracks up into smaller, useable pieces, you can encounter a certain natural resistance in yourself. This largely stems from the feeling that your track as it stands is an organic whole. Consequently, to snip it up is like trying to chop a tree into smaller pieces. No matter how hard we try, we just cannot convince ourselves that those chopped up pieces offer a reflection of that original tree.

CUT-DOWNS AS FRACTALS

You will save yourself a good deal of annoyance and wasted time by looking at your cut-downs from a different standpoint. Rather than viewing them as chopped up pieces of your original work, try thinking of them instead as fractals of a whole.

A fractal is a pattern whose parts are reflections of that same pattern on a smaller or larger scale. It is an entirely natural way of organizing a system, with many examples in the natural world, such as ferns, whose smaller fronds radiate symmetrically out from a central stem whilst following the same shape as the complete fern.

Thinking of cut-downs as fractals of the whole will mean that they retain the sense of being complete tracks in their own right, despite being much shorter than the original. This attitude is essential because one of the integral features of cut-downs is that they have a logical sense of beginning and ending, just like any other piece of music. As such, when we create cut-downs, we don't simply chop up our piece into smaller segments. We have to re-compose it within the constraints of the required length. This amounts to a shrinking of the scale of the original piece rather than a division of it.

However, this does not solve all of our problems. Cut-down lengths are not only very specific, but the techniques that can be used to create them are somewhat limited. For example, due to the particular tempo and time signature of your track, it may be the case that your desired cut-down duration (15 seconds for example) turns out to be a rather awkward length of five bars and three beats. It is essential that each cut-down functions as a complete all-round piece of music in its own right - yet how often does a self-contained piece of music last for only five bars and three beats?

CREATING A CUT-DOWN

Despite such problems, production music composers routinely create effective cut-downs from an original piece of music. This is because they have realized that the essential art of the cut-down comes down to recomposition and as such, it is simply a matter of reflecting upon the essential compositional content of the track and examining the ways in which that content might then be logically reassembled into a shorter version of the original.

Practically speaking, the best way to go about this is to open up the file of the track and select 'Save As', using the same name plus a numeric tag indicating the number of seconds for the cut-down - such as '60s' - and save the new version. This ensures you can create your first cut-down safe in the knowledge that the original is still intact.

Once this is done, spend some time listening to the track as a whole to identify its essentials. In other words, what important elements need to be retained in order for the track to keep its identity and character? A good example of this would be the main theme of the track, which will often provide the core around which you will build your cut-down.

Now examine how many bars in length your theme is. Themes often tend to be constructed in nicely balanced four, eight, or sixteen bar chunks. Therefore, if your theme lasts for sixteen bars of 4/4 time at 80 beats per minute, it will last for a total of 48 seconds. As the central feature of your 60 second cut-down, this would then leave you with twelve seconds that could then be used for any intro or fill material that the track as an original whole uses.

Regardless of the techniques you use to manage this particular problem, the point being made is that it is manageable. It is just a matter of treating your musical material in a flexible and adaptable way.

A little bit of anticipation during the composition and recording of your original track can also go a long way towards helping you when it comes to preparing cut-downs. For example, creating a strong ending to your original track will always put you in a good position since it then allows you to work backwards when putting your cut-down together. Simply set your ending to the end of the allotted time, fill in the main melody, and then finally add any intros or fills in the limited space that remains at the beginning.

Once you have completed your sixty-second cut down you can then begin work on the thirty-second cut-down.

To do this, re-open the original file and then re-save it with the same track name added to which will be the tag '30s'. Alternatively, if you think the 60s version is more suitable for this purpose, re-save it in a '30s' form in order to start work on your 30 second cut-down.

This process will then continue right down to the level of the five second sting. At this point, your task will then be to accomplish what at first sight seems impossible: to reduce a full 2:28 track down to a comparatively minuscule length of five seconds.

This can be done providing you are prepared to be flexible and that you do not actually try to achieve the impossible. A simple example of this would be say, a slow piece for string orchestra. When reduced to a five second sting your cut-down may end up as being no more than a single string chord sustained for four seconds, leaving one second over for the reverb tail (see below). When doing this, do not feel disheartened. Surprising as it may seem, stings of this type are used quite often in television programmes, particularly nature documentaries.

CUTTING REVERB TAILS

Cut-downs have to be very exact. So exact that there can be no sound whatsoever beyond the cut-down length. In other words, for the 60 second version there is a strict 60 second cut-off point. Because of this you have to be very careful about the insidious effects of reverb, sustain or delay tails, that may end a couple of seconds after a sound has been triggered on the sequencer.

Bear in mind that although your sequencer might show that the notes of a chord have ended at the sixty-second mark, those notes as written do not include these tails. For this reason, any tails need to be cut-off precisely at the sixty second point.

Because of this most production music composers try to fit all of the sounds into the required length – minus a single second. A sixty-second cut-down will thus last for fifty-nine seconds, the final second being left for the reverb, sustain or delay tail. If the tail then goes beyond this point, sequencer automation is used in order to reduce it to zero at the required cut-off point.

In doing so, try not to create a dead zone on the audio file of the track. This is where a cut has been made of a reverb tail that then leaves a very conspicuous silence. In order to avoid these, use automation to gradually reduce the volume of the tail within the allotted one second time period. See Fig. 9. for an illustration of this.

Automated reduction to zero:

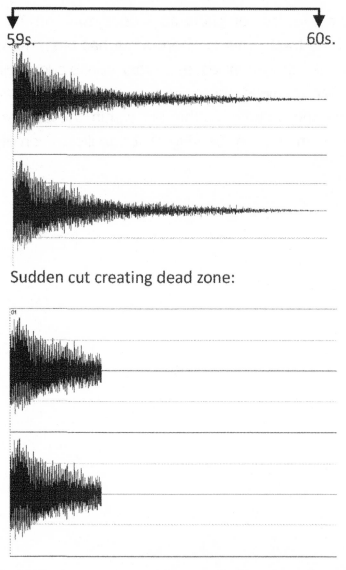

Sudden cut creating dead zone:

Fig. 9: *At the top can be seen an audio file where the reverb tail has been automated so that it reduces naturally. At the bottom is where it has been cut off leading a dead zone on the audio file.*

Having looked at some of the main features relevant to the creation of production music, we will now consider the production music libraries to whom we will be sending our music.

8: Music Libraries

Production music libraries are registered companies that have been specifically set up in order to sell and license production music to their clients. There are a substantial number of major libraries who work with many of the most prestigious television and media clients around the world.

There are also a host of smaller libraries that tend to cater for more niche markets. These may be run by a group of composers who do most of the work, but contract some of it out to other composers when they get stretched. Although less well-known than some of the major libraries, these smaller companies are still an essential part of a now thriving marketplace.

Well-known examples of major production music libraries are Audio Network, Sonoton, ImageM and De Wolfe. Each of these libraries has their own database of music available for licensing. Formerly, many of these libraries distributed themed CD albums to clients (for example 'Sports Jingles 3') although this distribution technique has now been largely superseded by more convenient distribution methods such as internet and cloud computing resources.

IMPORTANCE OF COMPOSERS

Without composers and producers to provide production music libraries with their music, their business model would not be viable. As such, the music provided by their composers is their very bread and butter. They need you just as much as you need them. When a library agrees to take your tracks it will therefore never be because they like you or want to do you a favour - it is because they know that they can make money from your tracks. And money is essentially the bottom line.

If a company refuses to take your tracks, this does not necessarily mean there is something wrong with your music - it could simply be because they do not feel they can make money from your tracks at that particular time. In fact, your tracks might be absolutely wonderful, but the library may already be over-subscribed so far as that particular genre or style is concerned. A different library meanwhile might be specifically looking for tracks in that style and consequently snap them up. In this respect, rather than trying to push your music onto a library it can sometimes be beneficial to take the opposite approach by contacting a library and finding out what kinds of music they are currently looking for.

SEARCH ENGINES

Music libraries tend to operate on a basic model: they take music tracks submitted by composers and store them on a database of tracks, usually subdivided by genre, theme or style.

A client who seeks music for their media production will search through that database and if they find some music they want to use, they purchase a license for the use of that music in their production. The composer then gets a cut of the revenue generated by this license fee. In fig. 10 you will see a flowchart that illustrates this distribution chain.

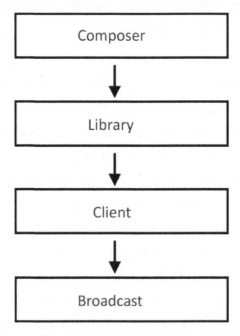

Fig. 10: *The distribution chain of a typical piece of production music*

One of the most important features of the modern production music library is its search engine. Whilst most major production music companies have their own in-house retail software on their websites, all libraries have a broadly similar search engine.

This search engine not only enables searches by track name, genre or composer, but by many other attributes designed to make the music search as quick and convenient as possible for the client and can include descriptors such as:

- keyword
- speed
- BPM
- duration
- words used in lyrics

- key
- time signature
- instruments used
- genre
- mood

It's a good idea to explore these search engines for yourself in order to find out more about the musical syntax used to portray the moods given. Pay particular attention to way in which they try to make discovering new music as intuitive and efficient as possible for their clients.

It is worth noting that libraries will normally collaborate with you in generating this information for your own tracks or simply create this information themselves, so don't waste hours noting down every possible attribute of your tracks unless you've been asked to do so.

You may notice that some libraries also offer the stems -

in other words the individual constituent parts - of each track for sale. This is so that if necessary, the client can then create their own mix of your track in order to better suit the particular context in which the music is going to be used. While composing you should try to ensure that you will be able to provide these stems to the library if required.

Having briefly looked at music libraries and the way in which their business tends to operate, let us now consider two features which are essential for the production music composer to know about: copyright and payments.

9: Copyright And Payment

As with any business, money is the most vital yet complex aspect of the whole production music industry. Because music can be easily duplicated and copied it is essential that the music industry is able to both buy and sell the rights to use this music in particular ways. These rights fall under the general subject of copyright.

In order to find out more about how money flows in the production music industry, we must first look at copyright law and those collection societies that have been set up in order to collect royalties accrued as a result of the exploitation of copyrights.

MUSIC RIGHTS

Copyright law is complex. Make up a tune and whistle it out loud. You own the copyright to the rhythmic sequence of notes of the tune you just whistled. If someone wanted to release that, they would need to record you whistling. This recording of you whistling your tune would be seen as a separate entity to the actual tune itself. That recording is known as the Master. It is this Master that would be released through a production music library, and it is this Master that would generate fees through the mechanical and performance copyright system.

As the creator of a piece of music, by law, you have the exclusive right to reproduce it, distribute it, publicly perform it and make derivative works. For a piece of music to be played on a television programme, you need to give a third party the right to undertake these activities.

These rights are boiled down into three broad rights:

- The Mechanical right – this is the right to create copies of your music, i.e. reproduce it.

- The Synchronisation right – this is the right to synchronise your track with a television programme. This is a combination of the rights of reproduction, distribution and derivation – but also incorporates the Mechanical right.

- The Performance right – this is the right to publicly "perform" your music – in this case, performing means to broadcast it.

Mechanical copyright is the right to reproduce a Master onto CD, DVD, or any other piece of media. Adding a piece of music to visual media (for example a television programme) counts as reproduction, and therefore a mechanical license is needed. The technical term for adding a piece of recorded music to visual media is synchronisation, and therefore in order to do this a synchronisation license is required. Confused? Just remember that a mechanical license is equivalent to a synchronisation license.

MUSIC SYNCHRONIZATION

Once this synchronisation occurs, the television programme in question will be broadcast with the piece of music playing alongside the visual media. Therefore, as far as copyright law is concerned, the piece of music is being broadcast.

According to copyright law, this broadcast counts as a performance of the piece of music, just like it would be if it was played live at a gig or broadcast on its own over the radio. Therefore, in order to do this, a performance license is needed. These licenses cost money.

You also need to know that as a production music composer, you will normally be regarded as the writer (or composer) and the library you write for will be regarded as the publisher.

To summarise the two main rights:

Mechanical Right: The right to reproduce the piece of music, also known as the synchronisation license in visual media.

Performance Right: The right to perform the piece of music, that is, to broadcast it.

COLLECTION SOCIETIES

With the thousands of licenses for the two rights that must be generated worldwide every day, it would be impossible for composers (and libraries) to keep track of this by themselves. This is where collection societies come into play.

In the UK, mechanical licenses are issued by the Mechanical Copyright Protection Society (the MCPS) and performance licenses are granted by the Performing Right Society (the PRS). In order to be paid royalties by these Societies, you will need to register with them in order to become a member and make a payment to each of them to join.

When a license is granted for the reproduction or performance of a piece of music, a fee is generated. This fee is set by the regional collection society. Let's take a look in fig. 11, at how these fees are generated when a track is used in a television show:

The MCPS knows to pay you for your music because a transaction occurred when the programme creator paid for the license, but how does the PRS know to pay you for your music's the subsequent broadcast of your music? The answer is simple: through cue sheets. A broadcaster fills in and submits a cue sheet to the PRS as part of the conditions of the license to use the music. The cue sheet contains all the information that the PRS needs to pay the performance royalty, such as the programme title, episode number, track name, composer name, and so on.

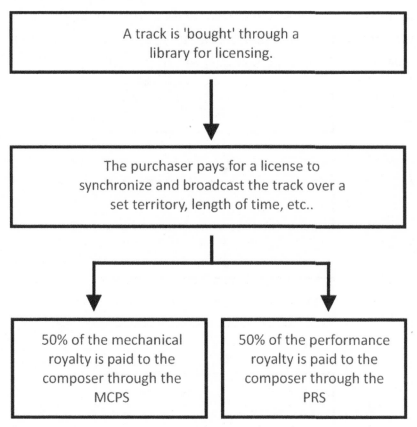

Fig. 11: *Fees generated when a track is used in a piece of broadcast media*

What happens if an overseas programme maker wishes to use your music? They license the music through your library's sub-publisher. While 'sub-publisher' is a technical term used in the music publishing industry, in this context we can understand it as being an overseas affiliate of your library, usually an independent library themselves.

The overseas programme maker licenses the music

from this overseas library, who makes the relevant payments to their overseas collection societies, who then filter this money back to your own collection society. This process is illustrated in fig. 12.

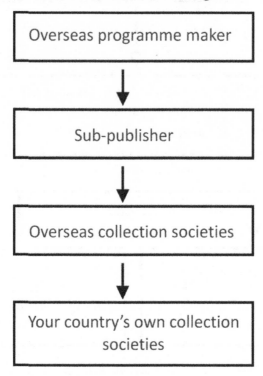

Fig. 12: *The flow of money from an overseas collection society*

Although the benefit of sub-publishing means that your tracks gain an expanded distribution, each link in the chain will take its own cut, which means that as the composer, you will then receive a smaller percentage of the license fee.

Moreover, this chain of cue sheets and societies, combined with quarterly payment schedules can make for a slow process, meaning that it can be up to a couple of years between a royalty being generated and that royalty arriving in your bank account.

Being a UK-based writer, I have written about British collection societies. However, countries all over the world have their own collection societies who operate the same model – examples include BMI and ASCAP in the USA; SOCAN in Canada; APRA in Australasia; ACUM in Israel; SADAIC in Argentina. These collection societies operate together as a network, making sure that no matter where in the world your music is played, the royalties generated (eventually) find their way back to you.

Whilst this chapter has dealt with how money flows within traditional production music libraries, there are alternate music library business models in existence. In the next chapter, we'll look at some of these models and examine how they differ for both clients and composers.

10: Library Models

Not all libraries use the same business model, so when choosing a library, make sure that it uses a model that you want to operate by. Generally speaking, there are only a few fundamental types of library business model. In the traditional model with which most of us are familiar, the library exclusively owns its music which is then licensed worldwide through a collection society. This means the collection society has set prices for various types of music use which are then paid to the societies.

In the UK, big libraries operate according to the fee rate set by the MCPS, the mechanical copyright collection society. Clients purchasing through these libraries have no choice but to pay these fixed rates. However, a new generation of libraries has emerged, seeking to undercut them. They tend to offer set fees for unlimited worldwide synchronisation of the track. The artist sometimes receives some of this, sometimes none, but they will receive 50% of performance royalties when the track is used and broadcast.

There is a third type of library generally referred to as royalty free. This is where a client pays a one-off fee for unlimited use of the music. However, this description can be deceptive, because broadcasters still need to fill out a cue sheet for their collection society, and thereby pay performance royalties. In this respect, these libraries conform to the business models already noted above.

However, these latter libraries circumvent the paying of performance royalties on behalf of their clients by contractually asking their composers to warrant that they are not members of collection societies. On that basis, their business model appears as shown in fig. 13.

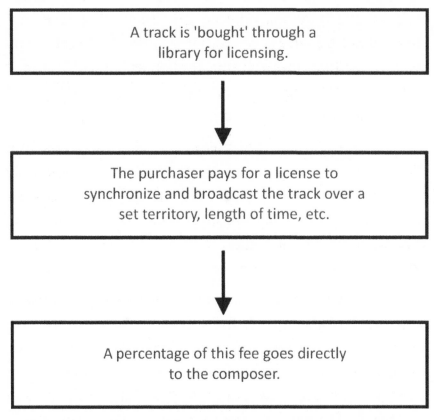

Fig. 13: *The business model of a royalty-free library*

These types of libraries are identifiable by their rock-bottom cost. Some even allow the composer to set their own price, and take a cut from this – positioning themselves as more of a marketplace than a library.

EXCLUSIVE LIBRARIES

Another important aspect of the library business model is the exclusivity a library demands of its tracks. In this respect, libraries tend to fall into one of three categories.

First there are those that work on an exclusivity model. This means they will only accept tracks that have not and will not be sold to any other libraries, or used in any work other than through that particular library. The vast majority of the top libraries and increasing numbers of smaller libraries have this policy.

One of the obvious advantages of this model is that although the library might have an effective monopoly over the work you place with them, other libraries cannot compete to undercut one another - and thereby reduce your remuneration - in the event of a client seeking the lowest cost for using your track.

Another advantage is that exclusivity allows you to work with the top libraries in the industry. Being at the top they have a larger and more diversified client list, thereby enhancing the chances of your music being auditioned, heard and used. Additionally, the library is incentivised to promote your work in order to retain you as a composer because you will publish future music elsewhere if they fail to generate any revenue for you.

One of the downsides of an exclusive library is that if your track performs poorly, you cannot remove the track to give it to another library, except by way of something called a contractual reversion clause. A reversion clause is where if your music generates no sales for a fixed period (generally a few years), you can ask them to remove your music from their library. This means that if your track is not selling, you have to wait that fixed period before triggering the clause, and until you trigger that clause your music is just sitting there, earning no revenue for either party.

SEMI-EXCLUSIVE LIBRARIES

A second category are the semi-exclusive libraries. Although these will not accept tracks that have a placement with other libraries, they will still allow the composer to put their tracks on sale within the general commercial marketplace. This model is sometimes used by smaller libraries to attract professional composers who may already have their own media contacts.

Some composers actually prefer to place their tracks with semi-exclusive libraries. This works particularly well for composers who write music that is intended for purposes other than library, but which is also suitable for use as production music.

NON-EXCLUSIVE LIBRARIES

Finally, there are libraries that operate using a non-exclusive model, meaning that composers are free to sell their tracks to other non-exclusive libraries. Non-exclusive libraries normally use a practice known as retitling in order to sell music on a non-exclusive basis.

This means that they will rename a track and report this retitled track to the collection societies, allowing composers to continue selling their track under a different title. In effect this means that a composer who sells their track through five different non-exclusive libraries will have five different instances of their track for sale, each with a different name.

An obvious advantage of the non-exclusive model is that you can diversify the investment in your track by selling it to as many non-exclusive libraries as possible, thereby increasing your odds of making a sale.

A disadvantage of the non-exclusive model is that high-budget clients looking for a theme or distinctive track are less likely to use a track that may be commonly available across several libraries. The risk here is that the track might also be used in productions that prestigious media companies may not want to be associated with.

Having considered some of the main business models under which production music libraries operate, let us now consider the process of actually choosing a library to send your work to.

11: Choosing A Library

For a composer who is new to the production music industry, being able to select the right library to submit their music to is very important. However, this choice is always difficult, especially in view of the fact that there are now hundreds of such libraries in existence, each of which may use one of a number of different business models. To discover which libraries to approach, it is necessary to begin researching them.

A useful list of production music libraries can be found upon the PRS' (Performing Rights Society) website. This list can provide the production music composer with valuable information about each of the libraries listed, including their contact details.

When evaluating the merits of a particular library, the strength of a library's client demand represents a good indicator. Put simply, this is how much money clients spend at the library. In order to estimate client demand, you will need to discover the library's annual turnover.

Assuming the library to be a limited liability company, their accounts (and therefore their annual turnover) should be a matter of public record within many countries. Furthermore, if the library is large enough, this figure may even be public knowledge.

However, it is important to bear in mind that if production music is just one strand of a library's many activities, or the library is split into smaller holding companies, the figure you see may not accurately reflect its library turnover.

Another aspect to consider is the tracks that they list. Do they have a section on their website detailing their bestsellers? If so, listen to them. If you've already heard these tracks on television before, then that's an indicator of a library with major media clients.

Next, consider looking at their overseas distributors. Are there distributors for all major music markets as well as emerging markets? Do these distributors appear to be successful libraries themselves? It is also wise to check whether they appear to have high-level corporate/venture capital backing (from a major music label, for example).

Ask yourself whether their website is well designed with an accessible user interface. Does it appear easy to contact their customer service representatives? A library geared for sales will always make this process as straightforward as possible. As a potential client, would you consider buying from them?

Using these research techniques, you can begin to separate the libraries you find into the following useful categories:

- Established independent giants

- Corporate-owned giants

- Up-and-comers

- Major royalty-free

ESTABLISHED INDEPENDENT GIANTS

The independent giants are the major players in the production music marketplace. Most production music composers aspire to place their work with this sort of library. Distinguished by their major client base and massive turnover, any tracks lodged with these companies have the potential to do well. This is because their policy is only to accept those tracks they believe there is a ready market for.

Because of this, all tracks accepted by these companies have to display the highest possible professional standards of musical production.

Four of the major players in this category are De Wolfe Music, KPM, Sonoton International and Audio Network.

De Wolfe Music operates under the cover of some ten subsidiary labels for which it acts as the licensing agent. They will accept demos from new composers - which need to be presented in the form of a link attached to an email - but they offer no guarantee of a reply.

KPM is an acronym for Keith-Prowse-Maurice, the surnames of the three men who were instrumental in starting up the library. Although the company has now merged with EMI, it still operates with a great degree of autonomy. They will not accept demos directly, recommending instead that new composers contact one of the various libraries for which KPM acts as the licensing agent.

Sonoton International is one of the most well-known libraries throughout the world. It acts as licensing agent for numerous subsidiary labels and like KPM will not take demos directly, but instead recommends contacting one of the libraries for which they act as licensing agent.

Audio Network is also a giant in the field owing to its very impressive client base. In spite of being a major UK library, they work outside of the MCPS' mechanical royalty system.

CORPORATE-OWNED GIANTS

This category covers libraries owned by a major label such as Extreme Music owned by the massive Sony/ATV Publishing Company; Imagem owned by the huge Canadian rights firm Ole; FirstCom owned by the Universal Music Group and Warner/Chappell. Being owned by a larger corporation means that these libraries enjoy a high degree of investment. They also have some of the most well-known composers in the field on their books, but it is not always easy to get a demo to some of them. Extreme Music, for example, do not accept unsolicited demos without an initial discussion via e-mail.

Imagem will take demos via a streaming link which you provide by email. They also require an artist bio.

Warner/Chappell by contrast, will not accept unsolicited demos but say that if you make enough of a noise on the scene they will know and as a result, will approach you themselves.

Up-and-comers

Up-and-comers are libraries such as Soho Music, Focus or The Funky Junkies which tend to host a smaller, boutique catalogue tailored towards niche musical demands.

Often building their reputations on a fresh, innovative approach to the production music market, they can be surprising in their openness to a more direct and personal approach.

Major royalty-free

Libraries such as Shutterstock, Stock Music or Getty Images Music operate on a royalty free model whereby the client pays a one-off fee for unlimited use of the music. You as the composer are then paid a percentage of that fee. As such, their main aim is to procure business by undercutting the major players, whilst simultaneously trying to attract composers who can produce high quality music for them.

Most of these libraries have a section on their website where you can upload demos to them. Unlike some of the other libraries that we have considered, they are always eager to take submissions from new composers. Consequently, an invitation to upload your music is often one of the most prominent features of their website.

LIBRARY REPORTS

If you want a secondary source of information on libraries, a website exists at the time of writing called www.musiclibraryreport.com. This site has a reasonably sized user base that reviews all the libraries within their database. This can be a very useful resource for a would-be production music composer. However, they do charge a fee for full access to the resources that they host on their site.

In the next chapter, we will look at how to go about submitting music to production music libraries.

12: Submitting A Demo

If you are serious about composing production music then at some point you are going to have to put together a demo of your music to send out to those libraries that you would like to work with. In this chapter we will be considering this process of demo submission, what it requires and how to go about it.

Your first task in this process will be to create a list of suitable libraries that you would like to send your demo to. When deciding upon these, there are a number of factors that need to be weighed up.

The first is the sense of confidence that you have in your own music. Do you feel that your music meets the high standards of music production required by the biggest and the best libraries? If so, you may want to approach some of the giants in the field. Or do you want to cut your teeth on something a little easier by working with less demanding libraries? If this is the case, then approaching some of the smaller libraries may be more suitable for you.

When deciding it is necessary to take into consideration not only what you would like, but also the likelihood of a given library taking your tracks. Your chances within the various broad categories of library previously mentioned are estimated in Table 12.1.

Table 12.1: *Chances with different types of libraries*

Category	Likelihood of success	Potential earnings
Independent giants:	Low-moderate	Medium-high
Corporate-owned giants:	Low	Medium-high
Up-and-comers (small):	Moderate	Medium
Major royalty-free:	Moderate-high	Low-medium

Observe that as far as the independent and corporate owned giants are concerned, the likelihood of getting your tracks signed is much lesser when compared with the up and coming or royalty free libraries. Offset against this is the fact that your earnings potential will be much higher with the independent and corporate owned giants than with the up and coming or royalty free libraries.

Which categories of library you choose to send your demo to will largely come down to your appetite for risk and how much belief you have in the quality of your tracks.

DEMO SUBMISSION PROCEDURES

Once you have gained a clear idea of the kind of libraries that you want to send a demo to, you can then begin making a list of suitable libraries. Because there are so many libraries out there, try to whittle your list down to around a dozen or so and put them in some kind of a hierarchical order, ranging from those you'd prefer to work with to those you may feel more ambivalent about.

Each library will have its own preferred demo submission procedures. If you are to stand even a chance of getting your music accepted, you must first submit a demo that accords with their specific requirements. You will usually be able to discover these requirements under a section of their website entitled Composers, Demo submissions, or within the Contact Us menu.

Ensure that you format your demo correctly in accordance with the stated requirements of each library that you intend to send it to. If you fail to do this your demo will simply be rejected.

Some libraries for example will want the demo to be in CD format only. Others will provide an online tool for you to upload your music. Some may require your tracks to be uploaded to SoundCloud, for which purpose they will then need to be provided with a proper link to the account concerned. Yet others will make it clear that they do not accept unsolicited demos. If this latter is the case, respect their wishes and move on – unless you can find a third party they work with, or stumble across one of their employees at a conference.

PURPOSE OF THE DEMO

Given that you now have a list of libraries that you would like to approach, together with a clear idea of their individual demo submission procedures, the next step is to prepare the demo itself. The purpose of your demo will be to show that:

- you are an industry professional aware of and operating according to professional industry standards.
- you are serious about your business.
- you can write outstanding production music.
- if the library to whom you are sending the demo to does not snap up your work, other libraries soon will.

For these purposes you will therefore need a portfolio of suitable production music tracks that you can send to each library within the format that each one has stipulated for demo submissions. You will also probably need an up to date artist's biography and a covering email. As all of these elements may be vitally important parts of the demo submission process no effort should be spared getting them just right.

YOUR PORTFOLIO

The portfolio of tracks that you are going to send out to the libraries will provide them with a great deal of valuable information about you as a production music composer. First it will show whether your tracks meet the professional music production standards that the library requires. If they do not, then no libraries are going to want to take your tracks.

If you are fortunate and the library recognizes the quality of your music, they may offer you some tips to help you get your music up to the calibre of music production that they require. If this occurs you should feel very fortunate because this kind of advice is priceless. Nobody has a better idea of what libraries want than the libraries themselves.

We know of numerous cases where this has happened, even to the point where the library offered constructive advice for as long as it took to get a particular composer's production values up to scratch. For the library this is seen to be a worthwhile investment of their time nurturing what they see to be a valuable talent.

Your demo will also show how well you have grasped

the production music genre. In this respect, the library is not going to want to know that you are a superb solo guitarist or that you can write epic albums. All that it wants to know is that you understand the language of production music.

That being said, some types of music adapt well for library purposes. If your music belongs to this category, the library may still take it because they recognize its potential as production music. This is why you will often hear albums of popular music from a couple of years back being used as production music. Having earned their living as part of the popular music chart cycle, the albums are then retired to library, where they continue to generate valuable revenue.

Your demo will also provide the library with a good idea of your breadth as a composer. For the library, an ideal production music composer would be one who could write superbly in any style or genre that was required of them. This makes the composer eminently useful to the library, especially when the library gets commissioned by a client to provide a variety of tracks in a particular style or genre.

This happens all of the time. A client may approach the library wanting a complete album of Cuban jazz, Celtic harp music or perhaps even Buddhist temple music. Whatever kind of music that the client wants, it is vital for the library to have capable composers on its books to whom they can delegate this work with complete confidence.

To be able to write music in a variety of styles is therefore very advantageous for a production music composer. There is however a risk to this. By aiming to master just too many different styles of music, the production music composer may become over-stretched, thereby leading to a reduction in the quality of their output.

Because of this, it is probably better in the long term for a composer to establish a reputation for being able to write superbly in those styles with which they are most familiar, rather than being able to produce mediocre music in a great variety of styles. As such, do not feel that you have to be the veritable master of all styles. Stick to what you know you are best at.

COMPILING A PORTFOLIO

Generally speaking, your portfolio should offer a fair and balanced representation of your general output as a composer. As such, you could even include up to ten or eleven tracks if that is acceptable to the particular library. Then again, some libraries may require only three tracks. Refer to the library demo submission process for guidance upon this particular issue.

However many tracks that you do include, make sure they display as much variation in mood and style as possible. If one of your tracks consists of an intimate acoustic guitar solo, there is no need to include another three tracks of the same ilk. To do so represents nothing but a wasted opportunity.

An exception to this advice would be that if intimate acoustic guitar solos are your specialty, then all of the tracks on your demo would then be fairly similar. In theory, there would be nothing wrong with this, providing that your demo then goes on to demonstrate the breadth of variety in style and mood within that particular genre or sub-genre of music.

You should also think carefully about the length of the tracks that you include. Generally speaking, try to keep your tracks down to a couple of minutes in length or so. The library can gauge everything that it wants to know from tracks of this length. In fact, the library will probably know whether your work might be suitable for them within just a few seconds of listening to your first track.

Another useful tip is that if you feel there is a variation in the quality of your tracks, don't try and hide lesser quality tracks at the end. Sometimes the library's A&R will deliberately listen to the last track first. The logic of this is that they know that composers tend to put their worse tracks at the end and consequently, if the final track meets the required standard, the library knows it could be on to a winner.

Although perhaps daunting, creating a portfolio of tracks to send to a production music library need not be a serious and solemn affair. After all, it offers a prime opportunity to bask in a feeling of hopefulness: the library may take your tracks they may go on to become their best-sellers.

TRACK LISTING AND TITLES

At some point your tracks are going to need to be arranged in a certain order and given suitable titles. Many musicians don't bother giving their tracks titles until they have to. Often some kind of a personal code is used, perhaps a combination of words and numbers i.e. piano 123.

This is because more often than not, modern music recording software requires project titles to be input before the project has even been properly started. So often a caretaker title is put in place that serves no other purpose than as a label of recognition of that project for the musician.

When giving tracks titles for library purposes, this will not do. Titles are a key part of the production music industry. Consequently, each track needs to be given a proper sounding title that not only reflects the content, mood and style of the music, but also serves as a linguistic attractor to any roaming clients.

In addition to titles, some libraries also require brief track descriptions. This is where, if you are not careful, you can make your tracks sound like an advert for incense or bath products:

'Luxuriate in the beautiful ambience of sonic sensuousness as tone and rhythm meet in a blissful cascade of shimmering bell-like sounds..'

Thankfully, giving our tracks titles and descriptions is work that we need not do on our own. If they are amenable, try enlisting members of your family and friends to listen to sympathetically to your tracks and convey the impressions, observations, suggestions, phrases and keywords that come to mind.

Being less personally involved in the project, friends and relatives can often offer valuable insights into the way that they hear and respond to your music and such insights can help you to find suitable titles and track descriptions. Moreover, done in this way, the creation of track titles and descriptions can be transformed into an enjoyable exercise rather than something you have to struggle with alone.

Once you have generated your track titles together with a brief description of each track, remember to include the precise length of the track in minutes and seconds on any track listing that may be required. As such information that may need to be provided for each track can include:

- track number - sequential order on the demo
- track title
- brief track description
- length of track.

Here is a representative example:

Track 1:   Streetlights and Shadows. Fast-paced edgy techno with discordant stabs. 2:28

Having completed your portfolio, you can then focus upon the other elements that may be required. One of these that you are likely to need is an artist's bio.

YOUR ARTIST BIO

An artist biography usually takes the forms of a short résumé of about a page in length. You may be asked to include this bio with your demo as an attachment to any email that you send to the library. When receiving email, nobody wants to be faced with a huge barrage of text whose main point is not even clear from the outset. As such, by including your bio as an attachment with the email, you can use it to give the library the option to learn more about you without your having to put your entire life story in the covering email.

Key information in your bio will typically include:

- who you are
- your contact details
- an artist's mission statement
- a brief summary of your experience
- your education

- anything else which you feel may be relevant to the library you are sending your music to.

If you have never done an artist's bio before, it is well worth spending some time getting it just right.[7] This is because, once it has been written, it can then be saved and sent as an attachment to every library that requests it. When tweaked to purpose, it can also be useful to send out to prospective agents, employers, and so on.

YOUR COVERING EMAIL

As your covering email might be the first point of contact the library will have with you and your work, it is well worth spending time composing a thoughtful email, one that is informative whilst being short and succinct. Think about what sort of e-mail you'd want to receive out of the blue. Consider including:

- How you know of the library
- Why you want to work with the library
- Why the library would want to work with you
- Your understanding of production music
- Whether you're open to editing your music according to their requirements

---

[7] There is some good advice to be had from MusicBizAcademy.com on this subject. The site hosts a useful article on writing an artist bio by music business expert Christopher Knab.

Before hitting 'Send' on your email, double and triple check it for spelling and layout errors and ensure that any links you have included to your portfolio - such as to SoundCloud for example - are actually live.

It is a good idea to place the bulk of the text of your email below the demo link, so that the library A&R people will have the opportunity to read your email while they listen to your tracks, but without having to wade through it before they can access your music. Once you are certain that all is as it should be, send off your email!

If the library requires your demo to take the form of a SoundCloud set make it private. That way you can count the number of plays you've received. However, this only works if you first play through each track just once. Having done so, this then automatically engages SoundCloud's analytics service. The value of this is that you can then use it to keep an eye out for when the library has played your tracks.

If you've evidently received plays, wait 48 hours for a response. If no response is forthcoming, send a polite follow-up email and wait for the same amount of time as it took for your tracks to be played after sending your initial email.

If you either receive no response to your follow up email or receive no plays within 4-6 weeks of your initial demo email, move on and begin this process again with the next library (although if you want to be absolutely certain, you could always call the library you demoed to and ask what their current demo review times are.)

The most important part of selling music to a library is to remember that it's no different to selling any other product to a business. The outcome is nothing personal: they'll take your work if they think their clients will want it and they won't if they don't. It really is that simple.

13: The Contract

Once you have sent out your demo and as a result, received an offer from a library, they will then send you a contract. Generally, the library will request that you sign two copies of the contract, one is for you to keep and the other is to be sent back to them.

Once you have your contract, get it checked by a specialist music lawyer if you can. Here it is useful to note that musicians unions - such as The UK Musicians Union - often provide valuable legal support for their members, which may include a dedicated Contract Advisory Service.

One of the main reasons for having your contract checked by a specialist is that the music business is filled with warning stories of dodgy contracts, hidden clauses and all sorts of issues that - once the contract has been signed - can be less than fair to the composer.

Another reason is the obscure wording used by contracts. No matter how bright you are, it often seems that the language used in music contracts was never written in order to be understood by the musician.

One of the best examples of this that we know of is a paragraph in the Grant of Rights section (see below) of a music contract used by a well-known music library:

"NOTWITHSTANDING THE FOREGOING IF THE WRITERS ARE A MEMBER OF THE PERFORMING RIGHTS SOCIETY LIMITED OR ONE OF ITS AFFILIATED SOCIETIES THE RIGHTS HEREBY ASSIGNED TO THE PUBLISHER ARE ASSIGNED SUBJECT TO THE RIGHTS OF THE SAID SOCIETY ARISING BY VIRTUE OF THE WRITERS MEMBERSHIP OF THE SAID SOCIETY OR OTHERWISE BUT INCLUDING THE REVERSIONARY INTEREST OF THE WRITERS IN SUCH RIGHTS EXPECTANT UPON THE DETERMINATION BY ANY MEANS OF THE RIGHTS OF THE SOCIETY AS AFORESAID SUBJECT TO THE PAYMENT TO THE WRITER BY THE PUBLISHER THE SHARE OF THE WRITERS PERFORMING RIGHTS FEES RECEIVED BY THE PUBLISHER SUCH SHARE TO BE NOT LESS THAN THE SHARE PREVIOUSLY PAYABLE TO THE WRITERS BY THE SAID SOCIETY."

I'm sorry, could you repeat that please?

No wonder musicians can become confused and even misled by the complex wording of contracts!

Because of this, when you're starting out it is worthwhile developing at least some idea of what you should be looking for in a sound music contract. With this in mind, let us consider some of the main terms that you ought to find within your contract, and what these will mean for you as a production music composer.

Please note however, that the authors of this book are musicians and not law professionals. Consequently, nothing stated in this book should be taken as legal advice, a substitute for legal advice or as an exhaustive account of everything you are liable to find in a good contract. The information that follows merely reflects the authors' personal experience of working with production music contracts. As such it is provided in the hope that it may be of some help to those looking forward to the pleasure of signing their first contract.

PARTIES

A contract is a legal agreement between the parties that are clearly stated in the contract. In the case of production music these will be the Library (and its designated representatives) and the Writer - which is you, as the composer of the music.

All of the parties involved need to be stated clearly at the top of the contract. There is also needs to be a list of the titles of the tracks that are included as a part of the contract.

A Definitions section may then follow, which will be used to clarify the precise meaning of certain terms, the territory in which the contract will be considered valid and any other such key terms that may need to be clearly defined.

GRANT OF RIGHTS

The Grant of Rights section is always enough to give any composer the heebie jeebies. This is the section where you willingly sign over the copyright of your music to the library.

However, this is all a regular part of the deal. If the library didn't own the copyright to your music, they wouldn't have the legal right to make copies of that music on your behalf - which is the whole reason you signed up with them in the first place. So without the composer granting certain rights to the library, the very basis for the library's business would then be null and void. These may include the right to:

- License others to use the music

- Publish and print the music or license others to do the same (if also a music publisher)

- Reproduce the music by means of mechanical reproduction (the mechanical copyright)

- Grant licenses for the synchronization of the music

- Make performances of the music

- Change the titles of the music if that is felt to be appropriate

- Alter, edit, couple, recouple and repackage your music

- Make other arrangements and adaptations of your track

- Use the writer's name, photograph, likeness and biography and so on.

The Grant of Rights section is a useful place to bind the library to certain agreements with regard to what they will do to exploit the music. Without such agreements in place there is the possibility that they could sign your music and then just sit on it.

Although this is unlikely in library, it can happen with record deals. Record companies have been known to sign up an artist for no other reason than to sit on their music. This not only prevents that artist from rivaling one of their well-established artists, but it also stops that artist from signing up with any other record companies.

When examining the Grant of Rights section carefully check the terms of any agreement regarding the reversion of the rights that the composer has signed over to the library. This is very important, because otherwise the contract only favours the library.

Ideally, there should be a clause that will state that if the library fails to satisfactorily exploit your music within a certain time period, or pay your royalties as and when agreed and at the amounts agreed, you are then free to cancel the agreement.

Libraries don't always put a reversion clause in your contract, but when they do, it can sometimes provide a way to rescue your tracks from a library that has completely failed to monetize them. We say sometimes, because it would be remiss to withdraw failing tracks from otherwise successful libraries, when - if you are patient enough - these same tracks may well begin to make money at a later date.

Another common feature of the Grant of Rights section is Consideration. This will state that the contract does not become binding on both parties - the library and the composer - until the library has paid to the composer a token amount of money which can often be as small as a pound or a dollar, payable in future.

The reason for consideration is that a contract is based on an exchange. If you granted the company the right to use the track without receiving anything in exchange, it wouldn't be a valid contract.

Although rare within the production music industry, some libraries will pay you an advance as consideration – a sum of money paid for the rights to your track. This will often be non-returnable and non-recoupable, meaning that if the track does not earn any money, the composer doesn't have to pay back the advance.

However, if the track does earn money, the publisher will first recoup the costs of the advance from these royalties and only begin paying the composer after they've paid themselves the amount of the advance.

WRITER'S WARRANTIES

This is an important section of the contract in which you, the writer, warrant that your productions are free of all and any encumbrances or claims. In other words, you are stating that no other legal party has any interest in, or right to your track. This is particularly relevant to producers who use samples in their tracks. This protects the libraries from the threat of legal action being taken against them due to any omission on your part. It will often tend to include key warranties such as:

- You, as the composer, actually have the right to sign the contract and assign the tracks to the library

- That the tracks are new, and have never been released elsewhere

- That the tracks were created exclusively by you, or, if it is a collaboration, that you own the right to sign it elsewhere

- That there has been no sampling that the library is unaware of

- That the tracks are not plagiarized

- That the tracks are not involved in any legal proceedings

- That the tracks aren't obscene or defamatory

- You agree that you indemnify the library against any claims that do arise from your tracks

- You waive all moral rights to the track, or agree not to assert your moral rights.

Your moral rights can include the right to be known as the composer of the track, or the right to object to any particular use of your track.

If you want to be known as the composer of the track, most libraries will be amenable to this. However, as a matter of expedience, libraries will still wish to retain the unrestricted freedom to sell your track without taking your personal moral stance on their clients' business into consideration. This is why the contract will request that you waive your right to object to any particular use of your track.

WRITER'S REMUNERATION

This section is the part of the contract that most concerns the writer, since it details how much the writer is going to be paid and in what way. This will take the form of an exhaustive list of where the library expects to gain income, including their exploitation of the:

- Performance rights

- Mechanical rights

- Synchronization rights

- All other income

In terms of royalties, the norm here is for a fifty/fifty split between Library and Writer, although a sixty/forty split in favour of the Library has been known to occur.

However be careful with this section, because it invariably includes a list of deductions that the library is authorized to make from the money that it pays you. This does and can include deduction of all sales taxes, collection society commission, agents' deductions, costs of manufacture, packaging, sales, distribution, promotion, artwork, advertising, accounting, and so on.

Keep an eye on this list of deductions. The money deducted should only be money that the library would never see in the first place, such as collection society fees, overseas fees, and so forth. If there are any deductions that don't make sense to you, seek legal advice on the matter.

Do bear in mind however that it is not in a reputable library's interest to charge you outrageous deductions to the point where rather than earning money you end up actually owing them - if libraries overcharged as a matter of course the policy would prove to be counterproductive since composers would no longer sign up with them. The composer's music after all, is their very bread and butter!

ACCOUNTING

A vital area that needs to be mentioned in the contract is accounting. The library needs to state clearly that they will keep clear and accurate accounts and records of all of the business that they do with your tracks. They themselves also need to be accountable to you so that you know that the numbers are in order.

How can you know this? You can only know if you have the right to appoint an accountant to audit the library's accounts. The contract should therefore state this. Although such audits rarely occur in practice, there is often a penalty clause placed into contracts, whereby the library has to pay the cost of the audit if a significant underpayment or inaccuracy is found.

TERRITORY

Your contract will also stipulate the territory in which it will be considered to be legally binding. So far as library music is concerned, the territory is usually global so it should say so in the contract: The World.

However, the music profession soon realized that by using these terms they might be missing a trick. After all, if the territory of the contract is defined as The World, what happens when we go on to form colonies on the moon - who will own the music then? - Heaven forbid, it will all be free! And when we finally get around to colonizing Mars, that will mean yet more free music! Because of this, you might even find the territory of the contract defined as "The Universe".

14: Conclusion

Once you have managed to place your music with a library you can then sit back and wait to get paid. This will usually be on a quarterly basis directly into a bank account of your own choosing. However, it is important to develop a realistic view of what you might receive for your efforts. To gain this it is helpful to consider the typical life cycle of a good production music track. For convenience, we'll use the life-cycle of a piece of chart music for comparison.

Generally speaking, the life-cycle of a chart track is rather short because a label aims to maximize sales within a short time period in order to attain the highest possible chart position (which thereby triggers further sales). We know of course, that chart music lasts far longer than a few months, because we hear tracks from the 1970s and 80s played on the radio. However, the vast majority of tracks that achieve long-term success are only those very few tracks that made it to the top of the charts in the first place and therefore have a place in the memories of the radio station's listeners.

Production music has an entirely different life cycle. This is because production music is mostly designed for the long term. In effect this means that a track has a life-cycle that can be measured not in months, but in years. Because of this, a single track can continue to earn royalties for a composer many years after it was first written.

STYLES OF MUSIC THAT ENDURE

One of the factors that can affect the life-cycle of production music tracks can be their style. Production music written in styles that might date rather quickly will obviously tend to have a much shorter shelf life than tracks written in styles that have proven themselves to be much more enduring.

Traditional classical is a good example of a more enduring style. Classical styles of music just do not tend to date. Audiences were listening to classical music a hundred years ago and they will probably be listening to the very same styles in a hundred years' time. Therefore if a production music composer writes a really good track emulating a classical style, that track could still be taken up by clients in twenty or thirty years' time.

Conversely, tracks written in more modern, niche genres, may have a much shorter shelf-life. This is because although a particular genre might have been very fashionable at a certain time, it often becomes exclusively associated with culture from that time period and therefore somewhat passé once the latest trend has moved elsewhere. Even the recent resurgence of 80s sci-fi soundtracks have been driven by tracks written in an 80s style using modern production techniques.

There again, if you write an effective track in a popular niche style and many clients want to use it, you will earn a great deal of money in a comparatively short period of time. Therefore it is often a matter of swings and roundabouts as far as style is concerned.

Be prepared for the long haul

Sheer luck can also play a large part. We know a composer who placed a track with an exclusive library and over a period of three years or so it was completely ignored. Then, to the writer's surprise, one year it suddenly featured on a large number of Christmas television programmes. In a period of couple of weeks, this one track thus earned the composer an unexpected but much appreciated bonus.

There is another example where a track that had been lying unused for some time was suddenly taken up as the theme for a major tennis tournament. In a couple of weeks that one track earned the composer enough to not have to work again for the year.

However, whatever the fluctuations of fortune, it is unrealistic to expect an immediate short-term return from library tracks, even when placed with the best libraries.

Composing for library should be viewed as a careful, long-term investment of one's time and effort. Even writers who become very successful will only tend to earn beer money for the first couple of years. Due to the inherent slowness of overseas royalty collection, it can take up to two years for royalties to reach you after they've been accumulated abroad.

Meanwhile, tracks from decades ago - that may have been long since forgotten by their composers - can still get regular airtime if their style and content have an enduring appeal. It's no wonder that production music is often known as a 'pension plan' within music business circles.

So how many tracks does a composer need to write in order to earn a full-time living? The answer of course, depends on the uptake of those tracks, but a rough figure that is currently quoted between composers is about 1,000 tracks over a mix of libraries.

One composer we know has well over a thousand tracks placed in library. However, because he writes under a dozen or so different pseudonyms it would be difficult to estimate just how many tracks he has actually created.

If you're lucky enough to write some bestsellers for one of the world's few top libraries, a few dozen tracks may be enough to earn you a successful living, while a few dozen more might make you comparatively wealthy.

However, first things first. In the short term, simply concentrate on getting some of your tracks placed in library and then see how they do. Even if you don't go on to write a great deal of library music, the music that you do manage to place can still provide a small income if it is successful.

In the meantime, the authors wish you every luck with you efforts to get your music placed with the libraries of your choice.

Index

image problems, 19
Imagem, 24, 117, 118
India, 54
individual outputs, 74
industry professional, 123
inherent value, 6, 8, 9, 18
insert effects, 77
instrumental forces, 24, 36, 41, 42
instrumentation, 25, 42, 45, 51
intellectual copyright, 9, 14
Japan, 54
jazz, 24, 29, 48, 125
John Williams, 44
jukebox, 10
Keith-Prowse-Maurice, 117
Kevin King, 4
koto, 54
KPM, 116, 117
less is more, 43
library business model, 109
library business models, 108
library client, 39
library music, 18, 21, 143, 147
license, 20, 97, 99, 103, 104, 105, 106, 107, 137
license fee, 99
licenses, 104, 105, 106, 137
licensing agent, 116, 117
light orchestral scores, 19
Locrian mode, 49
Logic, 22, 30
low frequency oscillation rate, 72
Lydian mode, 49
mainstream channels, 13
mainstream pop music, 20

major mode, 47, 48
marketing platform, 3
marketplace, 5, 6, 7, 11, 13, 15, 19, 97, 111, 112, 116
master output track, 75
master outputs, 74, 77, 84
master recording, 27
mastering, 74, 84, 85
mastering service, 84
mechanical copyright, 11, 14, 103, 137
Mechanical Copyright Protection Society, 105
mechanical license, 104
media houses, 13
media production companies, 13
media productions, 18, 20, 31, 37
melodic minor mode, 48
melodic modes, 46
melodic movement, 45
melody, 45, 50, 56, 64, 92
micro-scoring, 17
Middle East, 54
MIDI keyboard, 3
MIDI protocols, 72
minor mode, 47, 48
mixdown, 74, 75, 80, 85
mixing, 74, 75, 81, 83, 84
Mixolydian mode, 49
mobile phone ringtone, 15
mobile ringtone millionaires, 15
modes, 46, 47, 48, 49
monothematic, 32
mood music, 18, 34, 40
motif, 44
music creator, 7

148

Made in the USA
Monee, IL
23 April 2022

95299793R00090